T0358546

*The International Behavioural and Social Sciences Library*

# OPEN EMPLOYMENT AFTER
# MENTAL ILLNESS

TAVISTOCK

## The International Behavioural and Social Sciences Library

# HEALTH & SOCIETY
## In 12 Volumes

To the memory of George
SNW
To my mother and
the memory of my father
PJC

# Contents

# Acknowledgements

If ever a book has depended on others, this has. The list of people to whom we wish to express our warmest thanks runs into hundreds.

The Department of Health and Social Security has supported successive constituent projects with encouragement and understanding; we were fortunate to receive so much help from Mr Ian Jewesbury and Dr Bryan Hunt. Our relations with the Department of Employment have been always cordial and we acknowledge with gratitude the co-operation of Dr Eric Sams, Mr John Curtis, and their colleagues. At each planning stage we could call on a consultative and reviewing committee composed of university and outside experts and representatives of government departments: to its Chairman, Dr Peter Sainsbury we owe almost more than we can say, and we are most grateful to Professor J. H. Smith, Head of the Department of Sociology and Social Administration, Southampton University, Professor J. P. Martin, and other members for practical help at different times.

Amongst our immediate colleagues we should like to thank Mrs Marian Shea, in charge of our companion study; Mrs Janet Marks, who held a short term appointment on the programme; Mr Peter Coote, who conducted the comparative study of sickness absence in a manufacturing company; and Miss Gill Rollings, who assisted in the analysis of the work records of Study D. Our excellent secretaries, Mrs Freda Jones, Mrs Robbie Horspool, Mrs Althea Edwards, Mrs Celia Mills, Mrs Diana Hodgkinson, and Mrs Mary Offord seemed imbued with immense enthusiasm as well as skill. We appreciate also the hard work of Mrs Margaret Symes when programming the early rounds.

But nothing could have been achieved without our collaborators. All research of this sort depends on respondents, but our collaborators were much more, contributing long comments and many hours of extra work; the most exacting work was that undertaken by the record-keepers of the D Study and preceding case studies. Thus we express our deep gratitude to the Remploy works managers, the employers of Sample B, and respondents from the occupational health professions, particularly the members of the Society of Occupational Medicine. They could not have been reached but for the help of the Remploy Personnel Department, the staff of the psychiatric hospitals, and the then Hon. Secretary of the Society of Occupational Medicine, Dr Archibald. Dr Suzette Gauvain and Dr Peter Taylor kindly effected our introduction to the Society. We are also most grateful to those who have showed us round factories, workshops, and industrial units. And we feel we owe a debt of especial gratitude to employees who consented to have their working lives monitored for research purposes.

Finally, we thank Dr Eric Sams for invaluable criticism on reading the draft, for which of course we only are responsible; and Dr Douglas Bennett, Dr Donal Early, and Dr Peter Sainsbury for intangible inspiration.

# Foreword

This book examines some aspects of the life of the formerly mentally ill person, whose illness has necessitated a period of treatment as a psychiatric hospital in-patient. The premise adopted is that for those able to undertake it, full-time employment represents the ideal solution for both the ex-patient and the community. Working for a living is one of a person's basic activities, and determines not only his income, but also his status, self-esteem, friendship patterns, and many other aspects of his day to day life. An employee earning his living and having a circle of family and friends is unlikely to make the many monetary and other demands which the community must fund from taxation.

This process of rehabilitation to open employment is to some extent hampered. Many psychiatrists have a limited experience of industry and view all industrial work as being repetitive assembly or packing on a fast-moving production line. They rarely think of clerical work in a small office, van driving, or stacking goods in a warehouse as being part of the industrial scene. On the other hand, many employers see mental illness as the madness of the film screen and know little of the careful preparation for discharge provided by the best hospitals, or of the modern regimes of medication which can stabilize a patient's condition. We attempt to bridge this gap by evaluating the attitudes and experiences of employers who have employed the formerly mentally ill. All previous investigations have begun with the ex-patient and examined his experiences in finding and keeping employment. In these studies the representative sampling of employees from hospital discharge records is straightforward, but the sampling of employers is never attempted. The method evolved in the course of our own research was to seek representative samples by sampling employers and then employees within each firm. There are many difficulties inherent in this approach. We discuss these problems in some detail in order that the results presented may be evaluated in context.

We present the employer's view of the ex-patient employee in both qualitative and quantitative terms. Sickness absence, patterns of behaviour at work, and the standard of work can be evaluated in fairly concrete terms. This information will be reassuring both to the ex-patient and to those endeavouring to aid his rehabilitation, as it charts what can be expected during this period of readjustment. Long periods of sickness absence rather than a sudden relapse are the norm, and even a sudden relapse need not spell disaster.

The reactions of the employer and the caring agencies to a crisis during the period of rehabilitation can be vitally important. We have described in the qualitative terms of simple case studies instances of good and bad practice in these situations.

Our objective is to increase the awareness of the various groups who are concerned with the central problem of the employment of the mentally ill, but none of whom is in a position to view the whole picture. There are the various arms of the medical fraternity: the general practitioners, the community psychiatric nurses, and the hospital psychiatrists who will find the employers' attitudes illuminating and perhaps be encouraged by their efforts to respond to the needs of the ex-patient. Social workers and the officers of the employment services will gain insight into both the medical and employment aspects of the problem. Many employers, employers organizations, and trade unions believe that they should help, but due perhaps to an unfortunate experience with a single individual, are unnecessarily apprehensive and unaware of the simple things that can be done. They will be encouraged to learn of the advances in medical treatment and of the many innovative schemes which ease the former in-patient back into full-time employment. More importantly, we hope that our studies will stimulate interest amongst those in training for the various caring professions.

We are mindful that our empirical studies are limited in scope and represent only a beginning, but we hope that others will be encouraged to pursue further investigations along similar lines.* Despite all the drawbacks we believe that the detailed appraisal of rehabilitation facilities, and the conclusions drawn from studying the experiences of over 1,200 ex-patients present information which will be of value to a wide range of people.

---

* Subject to the approval of the DHSS, the data and supporting documents are available from the Social Science Research Council Survey Archive at the University of Essex.

# I

## Why work?

This book is about people who have suffered psychiatric breakdown and the work they have subsequently done. There are many divisions of opinion about the nature and value of work as experienced by employees in industrial societies. To those who embrace the protestant ethic, it can be a passport to heaven. To those who subscribe to the conclusions of the sociologist Robert Dubin (1956), it is not a central life interest at all. Probably of more relevance to a discussion of the value of work for mentally ill people are the findings of those who have researched the concept of job satisfaction. One salient point is that job satisfaction in the intrinsic nature of work itself has been found to vary with occupation and social class; Blauner (1960) listing the percentages of workers who, given the chance, would choose the same work again, reported that over 80 per cent of mathematicians, lawyers, and journalists would do so, compared with under 22 per cent of unskilled car and steel workers. If such findings are related to the resettlement of mentally ill people, it is unrealistic to expect ex-patients from Social Class V to revel in the nature of the unskilled work that may have been found for them, when this is not the common reaction of their healthy fellows. But, and this is important, this is not to say that they may not derive overriding satisfaction from the mere fact of working at all. Theorists will recognize that for them, as for many low-skilled workers, a job will carry John Goldthorpe's (1968) 'instrumental' value; that is to say, it will be the instrument whereby they are able to provide themselves with compensating satisfactions, whether by purchasing goods or services or by financing the pursuit of alternative interests outside work. The first reason, then, why mentally ill people need to work is the same as it is for everybody; to procure themselves cash and satisfaction.

## Work as evidence of status and of recovery

A second reason may be adduced.

In many follow-up studies in the literature of psychiatric re-habilitation, employment has figured as a variable in the assessment of clinical progress. But to be in work is not only a variable, an indirect attribute for judging a patient's wellness otherwise defined. In the context of holding down a job in open employment, working is an end in itself as well as a means. In a very real sense a patient *is* well if he can hold down a job. No one has put this more clearly than Olshansky, writing in Massachusetts twenty years ago.

What does the American, or European ex-patient specifically gain by working? Olshansky and Unterberger write:

'First, of course, he acquires some self-esteem in his identification as a worker, and in meeting a social expectation. In a culture which places a low value on dependency, becoming self-supporting is important. Second, it provides a way of shedding one's patienthood and joining the homogeneous population of workers and non-patients. In our society, idleness has to be explained. By working, one can avoid the issue of one's past hospitalisation.

Third, work provides a means of denying one's illness and avoiding the threat of re-hospitalisation. As long as one continued to work, one's normality will be accepted by oneself as well as by significant others. Work becomes a visible measure of normality – in fact there are few other visible means available to the ex-patient to "prove" his wellness.

Fourth, work provides opportunity for being busy and having something to do. This need to do something is especially important for persons with limited internal resources and limited interests in leisuretime activities.

What would be the alternative to working? The fact is that many fear idleness because without work they would "feel lost," "go crazy," "feel useless," "feel bored," and many would not know what to do with their time. Thus, idleness would confront them with themselves, which many would find intolerable, for work compels attention to the outside realities and abandonment of one's fantasies, which tend to flourish when external demands are not pressing and ever-present. It provides a major bulwark and against the tendencies toward regression. Finally, it provides ties to others, regardless of one's tendency to isolation and withdrawal. Despite one's temperamental disposition, some contact with others is unavoidable. Thus, work provides a minimum of social participation they can enter into and

accept. For some, work is their central life activity and only interest, and if work is taken away, for whatever reason, they are face to face with a real crisis.'
(Olshansky and Unterberger 1963)

In the face of such an imposing catalogue of benefits, why is it that psychiatrists as a profession are not united in seeking them for their patients? For there is no doubt that most psychiatrists are simply not interested in work, either as a therapy or as an end in itself.

This point is of such central importance to the theme of this book that it is worth considering it in some detail.

In our view, the crux of the matter, as once again Olshansky emphasized, is that psychiatrists tend to see recovery in terms of insight following treatment rather than through what has been called the 'ego-preservative function of work'. Significantly, it was not a British doctor but a British sociologist, Baroness Wootton (1959), who incorporated the idea of work in her definition of mental health as: 'The ability to hold a job, have a family, keep out of trouble with the law, and enjoy the usual opportunities for pleasure.' Furthermore, it was a doctor, the research psychiatrist Douglas Bennett (1975), who confessed how hard it is for doctors and nurses to look favourably on work, believing that the sick need rest, not labour; and from ignorance, tending to equate all work with assembly lines and piecework.

On reflection, this is not surprising. The intellectual equipment of the psychiatrist, curious about people's emotions and actions, evidently differs from that of the industrial manager, skilled in technology or accountancy. The fact that the proportion of overseas doctors in psychiatry had by 1972 reached over 50 per cent must also be relevant. For an overseas doctor to become effectively involved with work would require that he absorb the unfamiliar culture of the factory and market place as well as that of the psychiatric hospital and health service.

For native and overseas doctors alike, ideas of work barely figure in the principal treatment options currently at their disposal. Pharmacology predominates; it is the discovery of so many important groups of drugs that has made possible the great leap forward of the last twenty-five years. Psychotherapy, though sometimes postulated as the alternative treatment to drugs, is in the practice of the average psychiatric hospital more often used in conjunction with them, and is delivered economically as group therapy rather than in the awful one-to-one encounter with an analyst. In neither of these two approaches is there much room for the 'ego-preserving function of work', and it is not until one meets a social psychiatrist, emphasizing the social component in so much mental illness, that the idea of using work as therapy is likely to find favour. Moreover, since the post of physician superintendent was abolished in British psychiatric hospitals in the 1960s, each independent consultant is free to follow his own judgement as to which treatment option he should adopt. One curious result is that an Industrial Therapy Organization may be supported by only a minority of consultants in the district. Again, a consultant in rehabilitation can set up a Rehabilitation Department to which none of his colleagues see fit to refer their patients.

## Work as therapy

We have just spoken of doctors using work as therapy. This is the third concept, the third reason why work is to be recommended in psychiatry. It derives from the fact that occupation, and paid work if the subject is capable of it, has been shown to impart a therapy of its own. This too is of such central importance to this book that the evidence for it will be presented quite fully.

The first two important studies, twenty years old but equally relevant today, are concerned with the life of the patient when he has left hospital. In this context, work may be equated with open employment. Cohen (1955) demonstrated the importance of employment in preventing relapse, by showing that when chronic schizophrenics left a Veterans' (ex-servicemen's) Hospital, their success in avoiding relapse was not related to the continuance of minor symptoms but was significantly related to their success in finding work, and that this in turn was related to the amount of vocational planning before the patients left hospital.

The second of these two major studies appeared in the *Lancet* in 1958, and was also an investigation into the post-hospital adjustment of chronic mental patients. Outcome was simply rated by counting staying out of hospital for at least a year as success and readmission to hospital for more than a month in the year·after discharge as failure.

All patients counted by this means as successes were rated by a scale of social adjustment, according to which one point was given for each of the following three items:

(a) being gainfully employed for five of the six months in the first year of discharge;                                        •
(b) being able to look after himself as regards appearance, dress, and use of money;
(c) showing adequate interpersonal relations, i.e. conducting him-

self without gross disturbance or violence on one hand, or without social withdrawal on the other.

The results showed up an important relationship between employment and success or failure. 41 per cent of the population worked six months or more, and of these, 97 per cent succeeded, whereas of the 43 per cent who were never employed, only 46 per cent succeeded. Of the eighty-nine successful patients who worked for most of the year, a third were rated as either moderately or severely disturbed, and many of the others had residual symptoms indicating that the presence of psychotic symptoms was not necessarily a serious obstacle to their employment (Brown, Carstairs, and Topping 1958).

Two later controlled studies which illustrate the role of work as therapy were conducted in hospital settings. Here, the work performed was the sheltered work of hospital industrial units, simpler than that encountered in open employment, though sharing some of its characteristics. One is drawn from the major research reported on in *Institutionalism and Schizophrenia* by J. K. Wing and G. W. Brown. This is a comparison of three mental hospitals, Netherne, Mapperly, and Severalls. Surveys were conducted in 1964 and again in 1968. The subjects were long-stay women schizophrenic patients, and the research method was a simple standard interview: on the basis of questions about attitude to discharge, life in hospital, general knowledge, and symptomatology, symptoms characteristic of schizophrenia (such as incoherence of speech) were then rated on a five point scale.

The importance of the authors' conclusion as justification for our own investigation cannot be overstated. The analysis, they found, brought out quite clearly that the most important single factor associated with improvement of primary handicaps was a reduction in the amount of time spent doing nothing, and that the only really important category distinguishing patients who improved clinically from those who did not was 'work and occupational therapy'. It was probably the introduction of industrial work at Severalls that accounted for much of the improvement there, in the authors' view. 'Thus inactivity appears to be one of the greatest dangers for the chronic schizophrenia patient and seems to be directly responsible for a certain proportion of clinical symptomatology such as flatness of affect, poverty of speech and social withdrawal.'

Another controlled study of relevance to the thesis that work in itself constitutes a therapeutic activity is much smaller in scale. Dr Agnes Miles, in the course of our major project on the whole subject of industrial therapy, investigated the effects on long-stay schizophrenic patients of working in two types of hospital workshop. One group consisted of twenty-six patients working in an industrial unit, while a group of twenty-four patients of similar age, length of stay, social history, and severity of illness worked in an occupational therapy department of the same psychiatric hospital. Dr Miles was interested in two areas, work and relationships.

For the first study, both groups were assessed according to two criteria: willingness to work and ability to work, measured at the beginning of the study and again six months later. The results were unequivocal and showed that the industrial unit was more successful than the occupational therapy department in improving the patients' willingness and ability to work, although there were improvements in the latter workshop as well (Miles 1971).

These same subjects were then studied by Dr Miles according to a third criterion concerned with the formation of personal relationships, an area of accepted difficulty in schizophrenia. By the use of ingenious sociometric techniques, through which even inarticulate patients could participate simply by naming a fellow-patient, Dr Miles found that the type of organization and the type of supervision prevailing in the industrial unit were more conducive to the patients forming relationships, and even incipient friendships, than were those prevailing in the occupational therapy department.

Organizationally, the work in the industrial unit frequently necessitated patients handing materials and components to each other; or acting in a flow-line or grouped assembly, perhaps with one of them packing the finished articles. Co-operation between the individual patients was vital, and positively required them to speak to each other.

Conversely, in the occupational therapy unit, patients were engaged on individual tasks, often quite different from those of the patient next to them. There was no need for them to speak, and the sight of a patient working alone, engulfed in a private world of his own, was more usual than in the industrial unit.

Comparing the two styles of supervision, Dr Miles found that the industrial unit staff treated the patients as workers and encouraged them to rely on each other, whereas the occupational therapists tended to regard them as patients needing help and guidance. It is clear which of the two approaches should tend to lessen symptoms of social withdrawal (Miles 1972).

The evidence just quoted does not constitute the whole story. Certainly controlled, matched studies such as these are the preferred research methods. But no assessment of the value of work as therapy would be complete without reference to the impact of the industrial therapy movement as it hit British psychiatric hospitals from 1955 onwards. Few assessments of this impact have appeared in the learned journals, though interesting accounts of the work done in different units are to be found in the nursing journals. Descriptions also occur in the annual reports of Dr Early's Bristol complex and of other Industrial Therapy Organizations at Epsom, Hanwell, Birmingham, and Reading, and the local authority centre at Croydon, also widely renowned. But the doctors who have concerned themselves seriously with industrial therapy at all, let alone with its academic justification, are few in number – hence the rarity of analytical studies. We shall return to this point.

Whether work will in the future occupy such a central place as it has hitherto in this and other industrialised countries will depend on factors outside the scope of these studies, and which include, for example, oil prices, third world economics, and the strategy of the feminist movement. It is also at the time of writing uncertain whether the 'new' chronic patient will prove susceptible to rehabilitative techniques developed in the 1950s for institutionalized but burnt-out schizophrenics. Whatever view one may take of such imponderables, the fact remains that society will still require a great deal of work on somebody's part to keep the wheels turning, and, demonstrably, ex-patients need their fair share of what is going, possibly more than robust personalities need it. The sort of work ex-patients can do, with least inconvenience to themselves and to their employers, is a topic which will continue to be of relevance.

# Dimensions of the problem: counts and characteristics of the formerly mentally ill

## Introduction

The first task is to attempt to identify and summarize, from official statistics and research studies other than our own, what is known of the numbers and characteristics of the group who form our focus of attention, namely former psychiatric hospital in-patients seeking or holding employment.

Some of the more straightforward statistics are available from data collected on a national basis by such government departments as the Department of Health and Social Security and Department of Employment giving, for example, the number of patients aged twenty-five to thirty-four discharged from hospital during 1972. However, these figures are unhelpful for several reasons. They are collected in a 'hospital-based' framework and consequently only provide information about hospital 'stocks', i.e. numbers present in hospital, and 'flows' to and from hospital. The breakdowns of these totals are available only by basic demographic characteristics, i.e. age and sex, by diagnosis, and by some basic administrative categories, for example, length of stay for discharges. Thus, it is the focus of the collection of national data which is unhelpful to us, rather than any intrinsic weakness of the statistics themselves. Although details of our population of interest can to some extent be deduced from these national figures, these deductions require many assumptions and will only provide a breakdown by the broad demographic, diagnostic, and administrative variables just mentioned.

The only other relevant data collected on a regular basis is that obtained when ex-patients come into contact with sheltered work and rehabilitation services, and consists of such partial items as the number of 'green card' holders, or the numbers attending day centres or sheltered workshops. If we are to assemble the type of detailed information we need, some form of special investigation is required.

## A model of stocks and flows

*Figure 2(1)* provides a schematic description which would be sufficient for our purposes.

Our particular interest is in the employment experiences of those who are former in-patients of psychiatric hospitals. This particular sub-group of the whole population would be identified if we were able to classify individuals in the population into a single category on each of three criteria, namely:

(i) age with mutually exclusive and exhaustive categories of: under sixteen, sixteen to sixty-four, sixty-five and over;
(ii) employment status, with mutually exclusive and exhaustive categories of: not seeking work, unemployed and seeking work, in employment;
(iii) hospital status with mutually exclusive and exhaustive categories of: no previous psychiatric hospital admission, currently a psychiatric hospital patient, formerly a psychiatric hospital patient.

Each individual would be classified into one category on each of the criteria. In theory it would be possible to identify twenty-seven different classes of individual, i.e. three categories of age × three categories of employment status × three categories of hospital status. But some of the classes by their very nature will contain no individuals, e.g. 'under sixteen former in-patients in employment', and some classes will be so small in number as to be of little relevance in our assessment of the overall picture, e.g. 'over sixty-five former in-patients seeking employment'. If we ignore classes which are redundant in either of these senses, then the classes that remain are:

| class | age group | description |
|---|---|---|
| 1 | under 16 | not former in-patient not seeking employment |
| 2 | under 16 | former in-patient not seeking employment |
| 3 | under 16 | currently in-patient not seeking employment |
| 4 | 16–64 | not former in-patient not seeking employment |
| 5 | 16–64 | former in-patient not seeking employment |
| 6 | 16–64 | currently in-patient not seeking employment |
| 7 | 16–64 | not former in-patient seeking employment |

| *class* | *age group* | *description* |
|---|---|---|
| 8 | 16–64 | former in-patient seeking employment |
| 9 | 16–64 | not former in-patient in employment |
| 10 | 16–64 | former in-patient in employment |
| 11 | over 65 | not former in-patient not seeking employment |
| 12 | over 65 | former in-patient not seeking employment |
| 13 | over 65 | currently in-patient not seeking employment. |

These thirteen classes are the 'stocks' of the model presented in *Figure 2(1)*. The numbers in any stock will change over time, but at any particular time it is possible to count the number of individuals in each stock.

When the model is set 'running' over time, 'flows' will be generated into, between, and out of the 'stocks' of the model presented in *Figure 2(1)*. Measurement of these flows requires that we determine their magnitude over a specified period of time, e.g. the number of discharges from psychiatric hospitals during 1972. Flows must always be expressed as rates or numbers per period of time. The verbal description given to a flow is determined by the stocks which it connects, e.g. first admissions sixteen to sixty-four not currently seeking employment.

There are many flows that could be incorporated into the model, but some of these flows will be redundant in the sense in which some stocks were redundant, i.e. the flow is either zero or very small. Other flows will be only of peripheral interest for our particular study, for example first admissions nought to sixteen. Besides omitting some flows between stocks, we have also omitted all the flows into and out of the model. The flow of births into stock 1 is of little direct interest. The flows of deaths out of each of the thirteen stocks are difficult to determine.

The limited available evidence on the differences in mortality rates by hospital status or employment status for a particular age group is conflicting. Wright (1975) argues that deaths from mental illness are insignificant. Whilst deaths directly attributable to mental illness may be insignificant, various studies have shown that more than the expected number of deaths occur amongst those with a history of mental illness. Clarke (1978) presents data to show that male lives with a history of psychoneuroses, who are accepted for life assurance, have between 0 and 39 per cent excess mortality over the assured population at large depending upon the severity of their previous history. These excess deaths are wholly attributable to two causes: suicides and accidents. Whilst 39 per cent may seem high it is small when compared to, for instance, the excesses of 100–200 per cent observed for those with a history of high blood pressure. Sims and Prior (1978) present similar

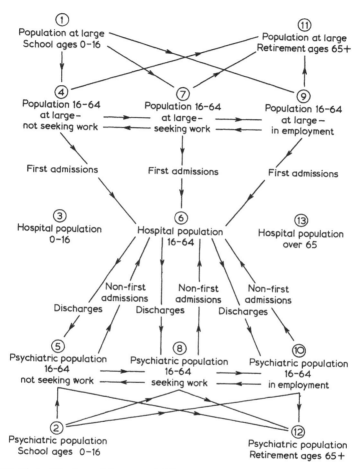

*Figure 2(1)*    Stocks and flows model for the population exposed to the risk of psychiatric hospital admission.

evidence in a study of 1,482 patients with a history of neuroses. The excess mortality observed was 64 per cent for men and 66 per cent for women. The excess deaths were again in the main attributed to accidents and suicide; although respiratory diseases for both sexes, diseases of the circulatory system for males and diseases of the nervous system for women also contributed to the excess.

Rorsman (1974) argues that it is well known that there is an increased mortality risk amongst psychiatric patients treated in hospital. This

*Open employment after mental illness*

evidence suggests that those with a psychiatric history have higher mortality, but we have no knowledge about how this varies with employment status. In the absence of detailed information we must make the rather sweeping assumption that previous psychiatric hospital admission or current unemployment does not make an individual of a particular age more or less likely to die. Thus, for any age category the flows out of each of the stocks will be of the same order of magnitude, i.e. the magnitude of each of the stocks will be influenced to the same degree.

We will attempt to deduce the sizes of the stocks and flows in our model from the available data for a point of time in the early 1970s. This date was chosen because our research programme started in 1970, and also because official figures often appear some years after the period to which they refer.

### The magnitude of the stocks

The 1971 Census provides details of the population of England and Wales by age, sex, and employment status combined for all categories of hospital status. The approximate magnitude of these stocks is given in *Table 2(1)*. Each of the values in the table is a combination of two or more of the stocks in our model.

Table 2(1)    *Estimated structure of population of England and Wales 1971*
(numbers in millions, distributions by sex)

| status | males | females |
|---|---|---|
| under 16 | 6.0 | 5.7 |
| employed 16–64 | 13.9 | 7.6 |
| unemployed 16–64 | 0.5 | 0.1 |
| not seeking employment 16–64 | 0.8 | 7.8 |
| over 65 | 2.4 | 4.0 |
| overall population | 23.7 | 25.1 |

*Source*: Derived from Department of Employment Gazette (1972) and Department of Health and Social Security (1971)

Recent figures (Grimes 1978) enable us to divide these combined figures into the stocks of *Figure 2(1)*. The tables published by Grimes are based upon first admission rates to psychiatric hospitals in England and Wales during 1975 and upon the then current mortality rates of the population of England and Wales. The tables are constructed upon the assumption that the mortality rates of psychiatric or former psychiatric in-patients are identical to the mortality rates of those who do not enter a psychiatric hospital. In order to divide the combined figures of *Table 2(1)* we need to make the additional assumption that the population is stationary, i.e. that current patterns of admission, mortality, births, emigration, and immigration implicit in Grimes' tables will remain unchanged into the future, meaning that the rates experienced by those aged forty now will be the same as those experienced in twenty years time by those aged twenty now.

Approximate breakdowns by hospital status of our three population age groups, constructed on the basis of Grimes' assumptions, are given in *Table 2(2)*. That for the population aged under sixteen provides

Table 2(2)   *Estimated population of England and Wales ('000s) mid-1971 by age and hospital status*

|  | under 16 | | 16–64 | | over 65 | | all ages |
|  | males | females | males | females | males | females | both sexes |
|---|---|---|---|---|---|---|---|
| population at large | 5,985 | 5,685 | 14,796 | 14,807 | 2,258 | 3,555 | 47,086 |
| former in-patient population | 4.1 | 2.3 | 456 | 623 | 174 | 361 | 1,620 |
| current in-patient population | 0.5 | 0.3 | 32 | 27 | 15 | 35 | 110 |

*Source*:  Derived from Department of Employment Gazette (1972), Department of Health and Social Security (1971), and Grimes (1978)

counts by sex of stocks 1, 2 and 3 of our model. The numbers of former and current in-patients are very small – less than one tenth of 1 per cent – and there are proportionately more boys than girls in these classes. In the population over sixty-five, approximately 7½ per cent of men and 10 per cent of women have been, or still are, psychiatric hospital in-patients. The difference is largely explained by the lighter mortality of women, and the higher incidence of certain psychiatric disorders amongst them. These are stocks 11, 12 and 13 of our model. But the breakdown of the working age population, aged sixteen to sixty-four, is that which chiefly interests us. It is estimated that approximately 3¼ per cent of the male population and 4¼ per cent of the female population in this age group have been or are currently psychiatric hospital in-patients. The numbers of former female in-patients are much higher than those of former male in-patients, but by contrast the current in-patient population of working age contains many more men than women. These figures represent stocks 4 to 10 of our model. Estimates of all the absolute numbers are displayed in *Table 2(2)*.

We turn now to employment status. *Table 2(1)* indicates that over 90 per cent of all men and about 50 per cent of all women of working age seek employment. It is unlikely that these proportions will prevail amongst the former in-patient population, but there has been no large-scale research to determine reliably the actual proportions. However, a small-scale unpublished study indicated that a few months after discharge from hospital the breakdown in a sample of size 200 was: 34 per cent employed, 9 per cent in sheltered employment, 23 per cent unemployed and 34 per cent not seeking work. A smaller study of male discharges aged fifteen to fifty-four showed about 80 per cent as having obtained employment at some time during the two years following discharge. The discrepancy between these two sets of figures must be largely accounted for by the fact that length of employment was not considered in the second study, and many ex-patients probably worked only for very short periods. The published data of hospital discharges do not help us to determine the sizes of these separate stocks, as the flows are described in terms of the source of continuing medical or social care on discharge rather than in terms of employment status.

Thus it is possible to attach magnitudes to some of the stocks of our models, but not, unfortunately, to those which constitute our focus of interest, that is the former in-patient population of working age divided by employment status. What we can and shall do in Chapter 4, is to make inferences about the ex-psychiatric population in employment, in so far as these employees are known to their employers. We know of no statistical studies of the whole psychiatric population not seeking work, nor of those unemployed and seeking work, which could be used to complement these estimates.

## Some characteristics of the stocks

It is possible to indicate some further characteristics of the stocks of our model in addition to the division by sex already presented. The most detailed information is available in respect of those who are currently hospital in-patients. We will confine our attention to the in-patient population aged sixteen to sixty-four.

*Table 2(3)* provides a breakdown of this population by age, sex, and duration of stay at the end of 1971. Men form the greater proportion of the population between ages twenty and fifty-five and the greater proportion of those who have been in-patients for at least a year. For all

Table 2(3)    *Structure of resident psychiatric hospital population in England and Wales,*
*1971*

| | | duration of stay (years) | | | | % male by |
| age | sex | 0–1 | 1–2 | 2–3 | 3+ | age group |
|---|---|---|---|---|---|---|
| 15–19 | male | 476 | 47 | 7 | 20 | 51 |
| | female | 477 | 43 | 9 | 3 | |
| 20–24 | male | 1,011 | 171 | 63 | 130 | 55 |
| | female | 878 | 107 | 33 | 106 | |
| 25–34 | male | 2,091 | 362 | 180 | 1,202 | 57 |
| | female | 1,875 | 272 | 133 | 571 | |
| 35–44 | male | 1,825 | 445 | 322 | 3,048 | 58 |
| | female | 1,968 | 250 | 225 | 1,677 | |
| 45–54 | male | 1,881 | 614 | 466 | 6,772 | 58 |
| | female | 2,253 | 532 | 309 | 4,071 | |
| 55–64 | male | 1,811 | 534 | 469 | 8,424 | 51 |
| | female | 2,593 | 640 | 482 | 7,283 | |
| % male by duration of stay | | 48 | 54 | 56 | 59 | |

*Source*:  Derived from Department of Health and Social Security (1971).

age groups over twenty there is a U-shaped distribution of duration of stay for each sex. This reflects the heterogeneous nature of the hospital population of working age at any time, comprising a transient population who stay for a few months, and the remainder who are long-stay. The proportion of the male population resident for less than a year is 28 per cent and of the female population 38 per cent, whilst the proportion of male residents of over three years' stay is 61 per cent and of female residents 51 per cent. The short-term proportion in each case has been steadily rising, and the long-term proportions have been steadily falling, with the advent of the policy of community care.

*Table 2(4)* shows that the average age of the resident population rises with the duration of stay. The average age of female residents is always about two years greater than that for male residents. The average durations of stay by age for male and female residents are given in *Table 2(5)*. The average duration rises steadily with age from about seven to eight months for those aged fifteen to nineteen to about thirty-five to forty months for those aged fifty-five to sixty-four. At all ages males have longer average durations of stay than females, the gap widening as age increases. About 70 per cent of males and 60 per cent of females have been resident for more than twelve months.

Table 2(4)    *Average age of psychiatric hospital residents (years) in England and Wales, 1971*

| | duration of stay (years) | | | |
| --- | --- | --- | --- | --- |
| | *0–1* | *1–2* | *2–3* | *3+* |
| males | 40.6 | 44.2 | 47.3 | 51.3 |
| females | 42.9 | 46.8 | 48.9 | 53.0 |

*Source*: Derived from Department of Health and Social Security (1971).

Table 2(5)    *Average duration of stay of psychiatric hospital residents (months) England and Wales, 1971*

| | age | | | | | |
| --- | --- | --- | --- | --- | --- | --- |
| | *15–19* | *20–24* | *25–34* | *35–44* | *45–54* | *55–64* |
| males | 8.9 | 12.6 | 21.4 | 31.0 | 37.1 | 39.1 |
| females | 7.6 | 11.8 | 16.7 | 25.1 | 31.7 | 35.6 |

*Source*: Derived from Department of Health and Social Security (1971).

Irrespective of their employment status, there is a limited amount of information about the stocks of former in-patients, the majority of it collected when they receive some form of out-patient care. In 1970 in England and Wales there were approximately 92,000 people under local authority care, 3,000 attending training centres, and 2,700 in residential care (Bransby 1973). These figures include an unknown proportion who will have previously received only out-patient rather than in-patient care. The Disabled Persons Register includes those who register voluntarily if their handicap is substantial, and is expected to last at least twelve months. In 1977 there were about 410,000 registered persons (excluding war disabled), of whom 35,000 were handicapped because of mental illness or subnormality (Mattingly 1978). Not all of these will have been in-patients.

There have been several population surveys (e.g. Srole *et al.* 1962; Goldberg and Morrison 1963) which have shown a correlation between psychiatric illness and socio-economic status. It is apparent that some psychiatric conditions are found more frequently in the working classes. The causal relationship in this situation is unresolved. Whether it is the relative deprivation of the lower social classes which leads to psychiatric disturbance, or whether psychiatric illness leads to a 'drift' down the social ladder is unclear. The classic study by Jahoda (1972) of the effects of unemployment in an Austrian village indicated that long-term unemployment led to the development of psychiatric symptoms. Thus, in comparing the working population at large with the working population who have formerly been in-patients, we should suspect that there will be a greater proportion of the lower socio-economic classes, and higher levels of unemployment in these classes. It has also been found that there is a higher proportion of separated, divorced, and widowed persons amongst the psychiatrically ill than amongst the population at large. Again, the causal relationship is unclear.

## The magnitude of the flows

Again, the majority of available information concerns flows to and from psychiatric hospitals, and is contained in the Mental Health In-patient Enquiry (1971). For reasons we have explained, we will describe the situation pertaining during the early 1970s, although the change of policy towards community-based care in recent years means that the nature of some of the flows will have changed markedly.

There is no published breakdown of the flows by employment status immediately prior to the move to, or immediately following the move from, hospital.

The published figures provide a count of the total number of first admissions to psychiatric hospitals of people aged sixteen to sixty-four. In 1971 there were 20,800 male first admissions and 27,500 female first admissions, i.e. about 1.3 per '000 males and 1.6 per '000 females exposed to the risk of first admission. The apportionment of these flows between employment categories requires an assumption about the incidence of psychiatric illness (necessitating in-patient admission) amongst those not seeking work, the unemployed, and those in employment. Unfortunately there is no concrete basis upon which such an assumption can be made.

In 1971 there were 61,200 discharges of males and 82,000 discharges of females aged sixteen to sixty-four from psychiatric hospitals in England and Wales. For approximately one third of both male and female discharges this was the first period as a hospital in-patient. This proportion is falling with the advent of shorter and more frequent periods of treatment in hospital. Readmissions to hospital from amongst former in-patients have been rising correspondingly. In 1971 there were 39,500 readmissions of males and 52,700 readmissions of females.

For both discharges and readmissions there is little information about employment status. Various small-scale studies suggest that employment status on discharge is to a large extent determined by employment status prior to admission. Unemployment on discharge has also been found to be higher for older patients, for patients with a longer hospital stay, and for patients with a psychotic rather than a neurotic condition. It might be suspected that a larger proportion of readmissions would come from amongst the unemployed former in-patients, given the evidence that unemployment as a situation seems to lead to psychiatric symptoms.

## Characteristics of the flows

The characteristics of the flows from the population at large into the hospital population, i.e. first admissions, are given in *Table 2(6)*. The distribution by age for both sexes rises too rapidly to a peak in the twenty-five to thirty-four age group, and then falls slowly over the ages thirty-five to sixty-four. The proportion of male admissions in each age group is approximately 43 per cent. The distributions of admissions by age within each diagnostic group vary markedly. The distributions for psychoses tend to be skewed towards older age groups with the

Table 2(6)   *Characteristics of the distribution of first admissions aged 16–64 to psychiatric hospitals, by diagnosis England and Wales 1971*

| diagnosis | average age on first admission (years) | | % over age 35 | |
|---|---|---|---|---|
| | males | females | males | females |
| schizophrenia | 33.0 | 38.6 | 37 | 56 |
| depressive psychoses | 45.8 | 45.0 | 78 | 75 |
| senile psychoses | 52.7 | 52.4 | 86 | 86 |
| alcoholic psychoses | 42.6 | 43.4 | 72 | 73 |
| other psychoses | 44.6 | 36.5 | 69 | 43 |
| psycho-neuroses | 37.1 | 36.1 | 51 | 48 |
| alcoholism, drugs | 38.6 | 38.9 | 60 | 63 |
| personality disorder | 30.4 | 29.6 | 30 | 27 |
| mental handicap | 35.0 | 35.1 | 46 | 41 |
| other psychiatric conditions | 38.5 | 37.6 | 52 | 51 |
| all other conditions | 40.0 | 39.0 | 59 | 55 |
| all diagnoses | 38.0 | 38.1 | 53 | 53 |

*Source*: Derived from Department of Health and Social Security (1971).

exception of schizophrenia, which exhibits the opposite pattern, especially for males. The distribution by age for the other diagnostic groups tends to be reasonably symmetrical, with a peak in the age range twenty-five to forty-four.

Wing *et al.* (1972) have used data from the Camberwell Psychiatric Register to examine the prevalence of first contacts with the psychiatric services. For both in-patients and out-patients, the rates are found to be higher amongst single and divorced people than amongst the widowed and still married and are also higher than expected in the lower socio-economic groups for all diagnostic categories. Treatment involving in-patient care varies by diagnosis, about 55–60 per cent of those diagnosed psychotic having been admitted as in-patients during 1970 compared to approximately 20 per cent of neurotics.

A comparison of each age group in *Table 2(7)* with the corresponding

Table 2(7)  *Characteristics of the discharges aged 16–64 from psychiatric hospitals England and Wales 1971*

| | | estimated average length of stay (months) | |
| --- | --- | --- | --- |
| age on discharge | sex | first admission | readmission |
| 15–19 | males | 1.9 | 2.2 |
| | females | 1.7 | 2.1 |
| 20–24 | males | 1.7 | 2.4 |
| | females | 1.5 | 1.9 |
| 25–34 | males | 2.0 | 2.8 |
| | females | 1.5 | 2.1 |
| 35–44 | males | 2.7 | 3.7 |
| | females | 2.0 | 2.7 |
| 45–54 | males | 5.0 | 4.9 |
| | females | 3.4 | 3.2 |
| 55–64 | males | 8.0 | 6.6 |
| | females | 5.3 | 4.3 |

*Source*: Derived from Department of Health and Social Security (1971).

age group in *Table 2(5)* illustrates the selected nature of those who are discharged with respect to their length of stay in hospital. For example, in the forty-five to fifty-four age group for males the average length of stay for discharges is about five months, whilst for all residents the average length of stay is thirty-seven months. Discharge selectively chooses those with shorter duration of stay, again an illustration of the heterogeneous structure of the hospital population accentuated by the policy of the 'revolving door'.

*Table 2(7)* indicates some of the characteristics of discharged patients by age. The distributions of lengths of stay by age and category of admission are heavily skewed towards short durations of stay for all groups. Approximately one half of all discharges in any group have been in-patients for less than one month. Readmission necessitates a longer average stay as an in-patient for both sexes under age forty-five. For ages over forty-five the average stay on first admission is inflated by the discharge of 'old long-stay' patients into the community, about 1½ per cent of discharges of first admissions and about ½ per cent of discharges of readmissions having been in-patients for more than fifteen years. About 50 per cent of in-patients are discharged to some form of out-patient care, 6 per cent to day-patient care, and about 30 per cent to an unspecified source of continuing care.

*Table 2(8)* displays some of the characteristics of the readmissions of former in-patients of working age by sex and diagnosis. The pattern is very similar to that for first admissions, despite a shift of each distribution towards the older age groups. The striking features are the low average age of readmissions suffering from schizophrenia, especially amongst males, and a similar low average for both sexes amongst those with a diagnosis of personality disorder.

Table 2(8)  *Characteristics of the distribution of readmissions aged 16–64 to psychiatric hospitals in England and Wales 1971*

| diagnosis | average age on readmission | | % over age 35 | |
|---|---|---|---|---|
| | males | females | males | females |
| schizophrenia | 36.9 | 41.2 | 51 | 66 |
| depressive psychoses | 47.3 | 47.8 | 81 | 84 |
| senile psychoses | 53.4 | 54.0 | 88 | 88 |
| alcholic psychoses | 46.6 | 45.8 | 87 | 81 |
| other psychoses | 44.1 | 40.4 | 68 | 57 |
| psycho-neuroses | 40.8 | 40.1 | 65 | 61 |
| alcoholism, drugs | 42.1 | 38.3 | 71 | 49 |
| personality disorder | 34.3 | 32.9 | 41 | 36 |
| mental handicap | 34.8 | 38.8 | 46 | 57 |
| other psychiatric conditions | 41.2 | 40.2 | 62 | 61 |
| all other conditions | 42.8 | 43.0 | 69 | 69 |
| all diagnoses | 40.3 | 42.0 | 61 | 65 |

*Source*: Derived from Department of Health and Social Security (1971).

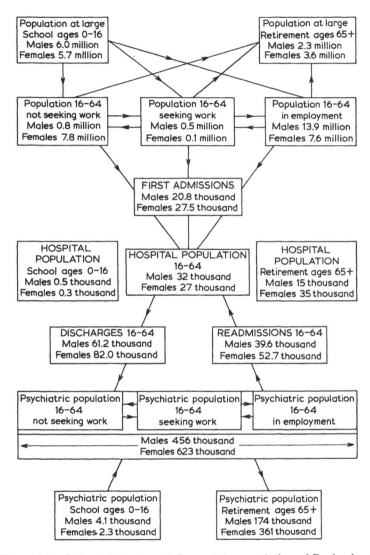

*Figure 2(2)*   Estimated stocks and flows of the population of England and Wales 1971

## The population under study

We are now in a position to attach fairly precise magnitudes to some of the stocks and flows of our simple model in *Figure 2(1)*. These results are displayed in Figure *2(2)*. Some flows are irrelevant to our purpose and have not been investigated. Only hypotheses as to the magnitude of others could be considered in view of the lack of research evidence.

Despite this quite searching investigation, the magnitude of the stock which principally interests us remains bafflingly indeterminate. We simply do not know, with the precision with which we know other magnitudes, how many people are in this group, nor do we know enough about the flows to and from this stock. One clue can be used to fix an upper limit, however. This clue is furnished by our knowledge of the proportions by sex of the population at large who seek work. Assuming that this proportion also holds true for the psychiatric population, then the maximum estimates for those in employment would be 400,000 males and 300,000 females. But since we believe that a smaller proportion of the psychiatric population seek work than the proportion of the population at large who do so, the actual figure is likely to be well inside this upper limit.

# 3

# Recent and existing provision for the rehabilitation and resettlement of the mentally ill by state and voluntary organizations

Historically, state rehabilitation and resettlement services for the mentally ill have evolved from services for the physically disabled. That is why the process has been so slow and the results so unsatisfactory. Mentally ill people were not deliberately excluded, they were simply not thought of. The reason was that in the 1940s, when the Tomlinson Committee was set up as an interdepartmental committee for the rehabilitation and resettlement of disabled persons, the public's concern was for people injured in war. At the same time the custodial care then available to psychiatric patients did little to suggest that they too might require rehabilitation services on a wide scale. Therefore, when the Disabled Persons' (Employment) Act of 1944 gave effect to the Tomlinson recommendations, a pattern of services was set up which has lasted without substantial overhaul for thirty-five years, during which the increasing numbers of the mentally ill have continued to some extent to be regarded as deviants, tiresomely refusing to conform to the standards of the physically disabled. One is reminded of Professor Higgins' sentiment in *My Fair Lady*: 'Why can't a woman be more like a man?'

What were the services established in 1944? The resettlement service, manned by Disablement Resettlement Officers (DROs) was charged with the duty of finding work for disabled people. The quota system laid upon employers of twenty or more persons a duty to employ a percentage of registered disabled people, and might be invoked by DROs in fulfilling their task. Industrial Rehabilitation Units, now Employment Rehabilitation Centres, were established to restore people to working fitness after injury, illness, or long unemployment. Sheltered employment, through the state organization Remploy, and a variety of grant-aided local authority and voluntary schemes, were provided for those whose disability disqualified them from open employment. 'Designated' employment, such as lift or car-park attendant, was reserved for disabled people.

On paper, the services looked substantial enough. From time to time they were reviewed. The Piercy Committee, reporting in 1956, recorded its impression that 'The facilities enabling disabled persons to get suitable employment [are] comprehensive and well established, needing little change or development'. It spoke of the 'completeness of the statutory provision which now exists'. The Committee's discussion of mental handicap (illness and subnormality) was slight and vague. Thus (para. 292) 'Patients who have recovered from psychosis or neurosis, and high grade mental defective patients . . . need the same kind of help as others in resettlement, aftercare and welfare services but there is a special need for close co-operation between the different services . . . Convalescent patients whose recovery is not . . . complete . . . need expert rehabilitation . . . .' Such generalized comment gets one nowhere. Yet too much blame need not be attributed to the Ministry of Labour in these early years. It was not then known that patients could be rehabilitated from residual symptoms of institutionalism. Indeed, institutionalism itself was barely recognized, for its symptoms can be taken for schizophrenia. Following the Piercy Report, the Disabled Persons' (Employment) Act 1958 made small administrative changes, but no major alterations in the services for the mentally ill or for anybody else.

The next relevant review was that of the departmental working party set up by the Ministry of Labour in September 1964, to examine the operation of industrial rehabilitation units (*Ministry of Labour Gazette* May 1966: 202–5), making recommendations which are still valid enough to be retained in the Manpower Services Commission's current programme; for example, for longer-term courses (*Ministry of Labour Gazette* May 1966: 205; and *Developing Employment and Training Services for Disabled People* 1977: para. 2.10). Unlike Piercy, the Working Party concentrated particular attention on mental disability, elaborating their ideas in an appendix to the main report. In this appendix the need for careful selection and suitable preparation of mentally ill candidates was emphasized, though it was recognized that 'there is no very reliable method of evaluating readiness for industrial rehabilitation'. The importance of adequate motivation was noted: 'in the short time available, the IRU cannot activate or develop motivation in a mentally handicapped person if it is not already there.' The authors of the appendix also commented on responses to rehabilitation by diagnosis, reporting almost total absence of success among psychopaths, a tendency to premature termination of their courses by psycho-neurotics, together with lack of staying power on discharge. Among psychotics, symptoms such as blunting of mood, disordered thought, and hallucinations, by now designated by Professor Wing and his colleagues as the primary handicaps of schizophrenia, were observed to be barely affected by IRU training, although some effect was noted on the secondary handicap of institutionalism provided this was not too deep seated. Lastly, a full discussion of the reasons for limiting the intake of psychiatric patients to IRUs justified this course by reference to 'essential group dynamics'. These observations were made twelve years ago, and it is legitimate to ask (in a way that it was not legitimate to ask after Piercy) why more has not been done to give effect to such insights.

A medical review of rehabilitation policy and services was under-taken in 1968 by a sub-committee of the Standing Medical Advisory Committee of the Central Health Services Council under the chairman-ship of Sir Ronald Tunbridge, with a membership which included two distinguished psychiatrists. Unlike Piercy, the Tunbridge Report was anything but complacent. It concerned itself more deeply with mental illness, around which the problems were increasing, for the Mental Health Act of 1959 had resulted in the loosening of legal constrictions and the not always discriminating discharge from hospital of many former patients.

Tunbridge's main recommendation was that hospital authorities should nominate a consultant psychiatrist to be in charge of re-habilitation in all psychiatric hospitals and general hospital units, and amongst other duties to be responsible for the industrial workshops inside the hospitals (paras 214–17). The importance of a carefully graded progression was emphasized, so that patients 'cannot make a sudden leap from a few hours occupational therapy in hospital to the full working week required in an industrial rehabilitation unit' (para. 219). Department of Employment evidence made it clear that many patients were in fact being referred by hospitals to industrial re-habilitation units prematurely, but 'in any event it is unlikely that there will ever be enough places in these units to meet the needs of psychiatric patients' (para. 220).

It is of interest that at this time the possibility of utilizing sheltered work facilities in the rehabilitation process, later to be recommended in the consultative document, was summarily dismissed. Sheltered work-shops, it was said, were 'intended for the employment of patients who, after adequate rehabilitation and detailed and careful assessment, are too disabled to have a reasonable chance of resettlement in economic work' (para. 221).

Meanwhile, the Department of Employment had decided to undertake its own appraisal of the relevance of its services to changed circumstances. Conducted by the Department's own Research and Planning Division, the review (1970) raised a number of important policy questions, and in accordance with current concepts of open government, consultative documents or discussion papers were issued to promote general debate upon them in advance of legislation. They formed an admirable series. The first, about the Department's resettlement services, appeared in July 1972; the second, on the future of the quota scheme, in May 1973; the third, on sheltered employment, in November of the same year; while the fourth, appearing in January 1974, was concerned with the provision of industrial rehabilitation and vocational training for disabled people. Lucid, well argued, well documented, supported by clear figures and tables, they provided ample ammunition with which to demolish outdated structures had sufficient impetus been present.

For what happened? Nothing. The statement in the House of Commons on 10 December 1975 by the then Under Secretary of State for Employment, Mr Harold Walker, had been long awaited, and it changed precisely nothing. The 3 per cent quota scheme was retained unaltered, despite the ruthless dissection of its contradictions in the consultative document. The insufficient sheltered work arrangements, so confusingly and variously operated, were left exactly as they were. Perhaps one feature of the Minister's speech may be noted with approval, namely his recognition of the rehabilitation potential in sheltered work. In the House of Commons debate that followed (*Hansard* 10 December 1975: cols 459–68), Mr Jack Ashley wanted all employers to pay the equivalent of a 3 per cent disabled quota, whether or not they actually employed them. Mr Maurice Macmillan pointed out that vigorous enforcement of the quota scheme might just result in more registration, not more employment. (He had a point. At a later date a drive on central government departments was instituted, and existing civil servants were reminded of car-parking advantages as an inducement to make them register and make the figures look better.) Mr Marten wanted the Queen's Award for Industry to be given only to those firms which fulfilled their quota, an idea commanding little favour. One part of the Minister's speech announced that responsibility for these services was to be transferred from the Department of Employment to the new Manpower Services Commission. This hardly seemed a dynamic innovation at the time: events will show whether a certain impression of urgency will be sustained. A flurry of further documents has followed the transfer, but there is as yet no sign of actual legislation to implement the proposals for reform which were first suggested years ago. Before these can be usefully discussed, however, we must review the provisions to which the consultative documents refer: the resettlement service, the quota scheme, the rehabilitation centres, and the various forms of sheltered employment.

## The resettlement service

The task of finding jobs for disabled people falls to the Disablement Resettlement Officer, or DRO, the central figure in the resettlement service. He is available to all disabled people whether or not they opt to be placed on the Disabled Persons' Employment Register, though approximately three-quarters of the people who seek help are in fact registered (Topliss 1975). The register has two sections. Section I is for people who on account of injury, disease, or congenital deformity are substantially handicapped in getting or keeping employment, and whose disability is likely to last at least twelve months, and these the Disablement Resettlement Officer will endeavour to place in open employment, possibily invoking the 3 per cent quota. The very severely disabled who register may be placed at the discretion of the DRO in Section II. These are potential workers who 'by reason of the nature of severity of their disablement' are (in the words of the Act):

'1. Unlikely either at any time or until after the lapse of a prolonged period to be able otherwise to obtain employment.

2. Though they might be able to obtain employment, would be unlikely to be able to complete therein on terms comparable as respects earnings and security with those enjoyed by persons engaged therein who are not subject to disablement.'

These people qualify for sheltered employment, whether provided by Remploy, or in a sheltered workshop, or in a sheltered industrial group – also known as an enclave – run by a local authority or voluntary organization. The minimum standard required of a sheltered worker has been generally taken to be one third of normal output, but it is admitted that at all times the register has included a large number of people who may not in practice be able to achieve this standard together with others not genuinely seeking employment at all. In 1978 the number of unemployed disabled people on the Section II Register totalled 12,899. In 1973, 10 per cent of the total for that year (11,164) were disabled by mental illness.

The Disablement Resettlement Service itself has been the object of strong criticism. But since 1970 a major reorganization has led to improvements which have not been generally acknowledged.

One such major innovation was to establish all resettlement work on a full-time basis. Hitherto there have been many part-time DROs, some of whom worked as little as four or five hours a week, the rest of their time being absorbed by their main duty as manager or deputy manager of a local employment exchange. The new arrangement means that the loose network of 1,158 DROs, 800 of whom had been part-time, has been transformed into an organization comprizing, by 1978, 590 full-time officers. On the human management side, individual aptitudes and preferences can be taken into account and fewer are press-ganged into a job they do not want. Most DROs are still recruited from clerical officers with experience of vacancy work at job centres and exchanges, but some are from the executive grade and a small proportion of the newest recruits are graduates. They are expected to remain at least three to five years in one job. The fact that the service is now organized by areas instead of by job centres gives scope for selection from forty or so personnel, rather than from perhaps the four or five possibilities at one exchange.

There have also been suggestions that the service ought to be more widely and flexibly available. Four DROs were therefore placed inside four hospitals (of which one was a psychiatric hospital, Mapperley near Nottingham) to counter the charge that they are so often consulted too late. The experiment was adjudged worthwhile and their number increased to fifteen, at which point the relevant round of financial cuts was announced and no further hospital resettlement appointments were made. The Department of Health are urging their reintroduction, for the officers have been accepted and welcomed by hospital staffs, but it is proving impossible to point to major successes in helping disabled people by this method. Another experiment in reaching a wider clientele has also failed to produce tangible evidence of its value. This was the extension of the service to the category of 'socially disadvantaged', defined for this purpose as 'those handicapped in obtaining or keeping employment by some non-medical cause, such as personality defects or domestic difficulties'. From 1973 to 1976 a series of experiments showed results so inconclusive that the project was abandoned.

Training is the last major area in which improvements have been sought. The National Training Centre, set up in 1975 in Leeds, has already trained over half the DRO total. The first part of their course is shared with the new grade of Job Centre Employment Adviser, after which DROs specialize for a further ten weeks, devoting a whole week to psychiatry, and undertaking field placements in hospitals for both the mentally and physically disabled.

These are considerable practical advances; but there are those, including some within the service, who believe that the disabled will never be served by a really committed organization until a complete career structure is introduced. It is also said that the present arrangements operate to the detriment of the more severely disabled, the argument for this view running as follows. The sixty senior DROs are all advisory, and are not the line supervisors of the DRO in the field. The boss of the DRO in the field is the local employment exchange or job centre manager: this too is known as integration. One goal of the job centre manager is to place as many people as possible, particularly in competition with the private employment agencies, and thus the DRO may well come under pressure to maximize disabled people's placings also, a goal more quickly achieved by finding jobs for easy cases than by spending time on those who most need it. Among the latter, inevitably, will be the mentally ill.

It will be evident that the DRO is the key man in resettlement, threading his way in and out of hospitals, rehabilitation centres, sheltered workshops, and the shops, offices, and factories offering open employment. At least he will be aware of the options, theoretically available, which will be discussed in the following pages.

### The quota system

Under the Disabled Persons (Employment) Act, 1944 employers of twenty or more employees have a duty to employ a percentage of registered disabled people; since 1946, 3 per cent. An employer who is below quota must not engage a person who is not registered as disabled, either for full-time, part-time, or casual work without a permit. This is how the law stands, and the consultative document explains why it is not only unenforced but unenforceable.

First, there are not enough registered disabled people to go round. A calculation in 1977 showed that even if all employers complied, there would be a quota of 2.4 per cent. Registrations have fallen from 906,000 in 1951 to 495,000 in 1978.

Second, it is known that many disabled people choose not to register – the official estimate is 50 per cent – and there is no evidence that disabled people who do register fare any better in their search for work than people who do not (Department of Employment 1973). Those with mental disability frequently prefer not to register; their handicap is not immediately apparent, and the advice of their doctors is often against registering. A survey of registered disabled men in seven companies employing 11,399 men in England and Wales, undertaken in 1970 by members of the research panel of the Society of Occupational Medicine, showed that only one fifth of men suffering chronic psychological disability were registered (Taylor *et al.* 1970).

Third, the obligation placed on employers to seek a permit is not enforced. The experience on the Continent, where Germany, France, and Italy also operate quota systems (but in favour of their war disabled) is that these governments also are unable or unwilling to enforce their statutory sanctions.

However, since the system persists despite these and other draw-backs – the administrative burden on employers and Disablement Resettlement Officers being a not inconsiderable one – it is worth looking at the present state of compliance with its regulations. In 1961 the percentage of disabled in firms subject to quota remained above the prescribed 3 per cent. By 1972 this had fallen to 2.1 per cent. Correspondingly, the proportion of employers not complying with the regulation rose from 39 per cent in 1961 to 58 per cent in 1972. There have been few or no prosecutions for non-compliance throughout this period, the Department feeling embarrassed at the idea of prosecuting private employers in view of the record of government and public sector employers.

The Act in point of fact is not binding on the Crown, but successive administrations have accepted that government departments should follow it in spirit. This they have conspicuously failed to do (*Department of Employment Gazette* November 1976, November 1977, November 1978). Of the twenty-nine departments, only the Stationery Office and the Mint have remained consistently above 3 per cent. The Employment Group had 3 per cent in 1976 but dropped to 2.5 per cent in 1977. The Department of Health and Social Security percentage stood at 2.1 per cent in 1976 and 2 per cent in 1977. In response to public demand, the figures for public sector employers were published in 1977 for the first time, and revealed a comparable situation. In local government, most authorities employed under 3 per cent, many less than 1 per cent: only a few of the smallest were above 3 per cent. Not one of the nationalized industries was up to quota; nor were the electricity boards; nor the regional water authorities. The area health authorities were worst of all. There are ninety-eight of these, sixty-four of which employed under 1 per cent and the remaining thirty-four between 1 per cent and 2 per cent. Not one had more than 2 per cent. One cannot refrain from remarking this poor showing of the health authorities, of all people, both centrally at DHSS and even more conspicuously at area level.

Meanwhile, with yet a further review promised for 1980, the

Department proceeds without undue loss of composure on the basis of these entirely artificial figures. They believe that the truer figure for quota fulfilment, if everyone were to register, would be much more like 4 per cent than 2 per cent. They profess to believe also that the political and educative value of the 3 per cent quota as an objective outweighs its mathematical nonsense. The fact that the unemployment rate for the disabled is twice as high as that generally suggests that there is still much need for this. An inspectorate has been appointed to scrutinize employers' records, a task previously performed by DROs in the field, who found that it did not accord well with their main task of placing people. As to the Government's review of its own policies on employing disabled people – about which the then Prime Minister Mr Callaghan gave a specific undertaking at the MIND Conference in October 1977 – one aspect is the need when recruiting to consider disabled people at all levels and not only as messengers and commissionaires. It appears that the Civil Service Commission is not yet wholly convinced of the rightness of this policy. Whether or not the issue to all employers by direct mail of a code of practice, entitled *Positive Policies*, produces any impact, remains to be seen. In any event, *Positive Policies* mentions the mentally ill once only in its eight pages of text, while four of its five illustrations feature the wheelchairs and adapted equipment associated with physical disability. As so often in policy statements from 1944 onwards, mental disability, though not excluded, is nowhere specified.

The key question is: how many mentally ill people are helped by the quota? But since no breakdown of the figures by diagnosis is made, this question cannot be answered. In the absence of such information, but in the presence of evidence of a widespread disinclination of mentally disabled people to register to be helped by it, the quota scheme's usefulness for them cannot be proved. One can only suspect that it is limited.

## Employment Rehabilitation Centres

Employment rehabilitation is to be distinguished (though not so sharply as is the practice) from the medical rehabilitation which is undertaken in hospital. It is run by the central government employment authority, at the time of writing the Employment Services Division, in the twenty-six Employment Rehabilitation Centres (formerly known as Industrial Rehabilitation Units) sited up and down the country. These have a total of 2,542 places, and in 1977, the last year for which full figures are available, 13,906 people passed through them. Mentally disabled people made up nearly 22 per cent of this total;

psychoneurosis 12 per cent, psychosis 6 per cent, and subnormality 3 per cent.

The objective of ERC rehabilitation is to make people as work-fit as possible following illness, injury, or prolonged unemployment: 'toning up' is a phrase the service likes to use. The centres are not vocational; they aim to restore confidence, help people back to a working routine, and provide expert assessment of their working capabilities. ERC staff should be well qualified for this, for occupational supervisors, an Employment Medical Advisory Service doctor, an occupational psychologist, a social worker, and a Disablement Resettlement Officer all conduct interviews and attend regular case conferences to assess each individual's progress. Courses last an average of seven weeks and are tailored to individual needs. A variety of occupations is on offer: machine operating, bench engineering, woodwork, assembly, light bench work, gardening, and concreting. The supervisors are all skilled craftsmen. Increasingly, there is instruction and educational revision for clerical and commercial posts.

The outcome for the psychiatrically disabled may be seen in the following figures extracted from the *Department of Employment Gazette* 1979 (see *Table 3.1*).

A fifth of all psychotics, and 17 per cent of people diagnosed psychoneurotic, failed to complete the course. Some years ago a departmental analysis of premature terminations showed that 50 per cent were attributable to medical reasons; 10 per cent to 'work' reasons; 10 per cent to financial, domestic and travelling reasons; and 20 per cent to disciplinary reasons, or because the rehabilitee was 'uninterested'. Of those that did finish, 36 per cent of psychotics, and 43 per cent of psychoneurotics were reported as being in employment or training three months afterwards. The average was 44 per cent; thus in 1977 some 302 people diagnosed as psychotic were employed or in training after their ERC course, and some 617 diagnosed neurotic, perhaps 920 altogether.

One of the most long-standing criticisms of ERCs is that the intake of psychiatrically disabled is limited to 20–25 per cent. This has meant patients waiting for weeks and months for places to become available – we heard of a wait of between nine months and a year at Perivale and of 114 psychiatrically disabled on the waiting list for Egham. One result is that ex-patients grow tired of waiting and swell another total which gives cause for concern, that of referrals who fail to take up their places.

When the Employment Services Division's own current research is published, the practice may well be modified. As part of the project, Professor Wing's Present State Examination (PSE, a scored schedule

Table 3(1)  Outcome for psychiatrically disabled of attendance at an ERC (1977)

| | (I)<br>number passed through in 1977 | (II)<br>number completing course | (III)<br>number not completing course | (IV)<br>(III) as % of (I) | (V)<br>number in employment 3 months after completion of course as % of (II) | (VI)<br>number in training 3 months after completion of course as % of (II) | (VII)<br><br>total |
|---|---|---|---|---|---|---|---|
| psycho-neurosis | 1,757 | 1,451 | 306 | 17.4 | 25.0 | 17.5 | 42.5 |
| psychosis | 833 | 659 | 174 | 20.9 | 22.6 | 13.3 | 35.9 |
| total all disabilities | 13,906 | 11,936 | 1,970 | 14.2 | 25.0 | 18.9 | 43.9 |

used to identify psychiatric symptoms) was administered to a random sample of rehabilitees with all types of disability. It was found that of the small percentage exhibiting such symptomatology, half had previously received no diagnosis of mental illness or disability at all, some having been referred for physical reasons. This finding quantifies what is in fact already known. Dr J. F. D. Murphy, EMAS doctor on the Egham ERC staff, has found the incidence of psychological problems to be high in the physically disabled, manifesting itself in long-standing anxiety, irrational fears, depression, and strong feelings of resentment (Murphy 1975). With the line dividing disabilities as blurred as this, it is not unreasonable to look for changes in policy which will acknowledge the prevalence of psychological disturbance across the whole spectrum of disability.

Another figure giving cause for official concern is the non-completion rate in psychiatric cases, standing at 17 per cent for neurotics and 21 per cent for psychotics. Many of the premature terminations are said to follow from the fact that referrals are misplaced, and this point has also been made strongly by Dr Early in relation to his Bristol workshops. ERC managers are said to experience great difficulty with psychiatrists who, since they seldom take the trouble to visit a Centre, have no idea what they are referring a patient to. Probably more doctors come from overseas to visit the Egham ERC, it was said, than doctors from the UK. But senior ERC personnel have confessed in their turn to having never set foot inside a hospital industrial therapy unit. The fact is that communication between the various agencies of rehabilitation – state, local authority, voluntary, and hospital – is so tenuous as to prejudice clients' working prospects.

Similarly, the Tunbridge Committee found that only 6 per cent of total referrals came from general practitioners (Appendix VII, *Table 4*); while one commentator doubted whether GPs and field social workers were aware of the existence of the facility at all (Campling 1976).

Other criticisms have identified the lack of evaluation of ERC methods of rehabilitation, particularly the method of follow-up. At present, a postcard is despatched to all rehabilitees six months after they leave, a system criticized as perfunctory and inadequate, leaving too many loopholes.

All these problems have been recognized by the Department of Employment itself. A research centre under the direction of Mr Paul Cornes has been set up alongside the large demonstration ERC in the grounds of Queen Mary's Hospital, Birmingham, to evaluate present methods. Two experiments at Leeds and Leicester ERCs are concerned in the rehabilitation of psychiatric patients. Their aim is to offer advice and help in an unhurried atmosphere before ex-patients ever set foot in the centre itself, since it is thought that in the past, psychiatric patients have often found themselves over-confronted at the outset by the demands an ERC course makes of them.

Thus, substantial effort has already been directed towards the evaluation and improvement of rehabilitation methods, and the first research reports will be considered with interest.

The above relates to mainstream ERC activities. There is also at Egham a special unit of twenty-four places named the Employment Preparation Section, set up at short notice and at headquarters request following the demise of the Industrial Therapy Organization at Epsom in 1975. The work done in it resembles that of one of the better hospital industrial therapy units: a small carpentry section, making children's wheelbarrows; a CSSD – or Central Sterile Supply operation; a goggle-packing job; and some simple hand assembly of electric plugs. Where it has the edge over a hospital unit is in its engineering section equipped with lathes and drills, in its more favourable staffing ratio, and in the payment of the standard training allowances.

Furthermore, the Section resembles its predecessor ITO (Industrial Therapy Organization), and differs from the ERC proper in the length of training period allowed, currently averaging twenty-two weeks and thus nearly four times as long as the standard course. This means that each EPS rehabilitee costs four times as much, and for this reason the Department does not intend to reproduce the experiment elsewhere. In any event, those advocating such a course have rather little to go on, since plans for monitoring the outcome of the unit unfortunately went astray. It is known, however, that of eighty-four referrals from July 1975, fifty-three were returned to their DROs with a recommendation for employment, twenty-two of these going directly into jobs, while thirty-one relapsed or terminated the course prematurely, results not out of line with rehabilitation experience elsewhere.

The past contribution of ERCs to the employment prospects of mentally ill people provides little room for complacency. (There is not even room for knowledge in the absence of a full record system.) It was their inadequacy that led to the privately-sponsored Industrial Therapy Organization movement of the 1960s, set up with the specific aim of creating facilities more closely attuned to the needs of mentally ill people. The establishment of longer training courses was one such innovation.

As to the future, other changes are contemplated by the Manpower Services Commission with the object of making ERC facilities available to a wider range of people, among them rehabilitees wishing to pursue a commercial career, and handicapped young people; indeed, possibly young people with no handicap other than their unemployed status (Department of Health and Social Security 1977: para. 3.33). All these ideas are fine provided they do not reduce the service's contribution to the resettlement of the disabled people it was set up to help, among them the mentally ill.

## Sheltered employment

Under Section 15 of the Disabled Persons' (Employment) Act 1944, facilities for employment under sheltered conditions may be provided for registered disabled people who by reason of the nature or severity of their disablement are unlikely, either at any time or until after the lapse of a long period, otherwise to obtain employment. Such employment may be provided by (a) the government; (b) local authorities; or (c) approved voluntary organizations (Department of Employment 1973a: para. 3.7). The financial contribution made by the Department of Employment varies with the nature of the agency arrangement. For the government body, Remploy, the annual difference between its expenditure on wages, materials, and overheads and its income from sales is met in full by the Exchequer, as are capital costs. The financial support available to local authorities is 75 per cent of approved expenditure on building and equipment, and 75 per cent of running costs, subject to an annual maximum (in 1979 £1,400 per worker) which is regularly reviewed. Independent voluntary bodies are grant-aided on the same system, with the difference that for them the percentage of running costs refundable has been raised from 75 to 90 (Department of Employment 1973a: paras 338–9). Examples of each type of provision will be reviewed.

### *Remploy*

The chief instrument devised by the 1944 Act for the provision of sheltered work for severely disabled people was an *ad hoc* company, Remploy. The company was incorporated in April 1945 precisely for this purpose. It was limited by guarantee, and without share capital. Because of the disabilities of the employees and the need to site factories all over the country, the Department of Employment provides the capital and makes up the difference between sales and costs. At the time (1972) when we were in touch with them in connection with our first survey (in which Remploy works managers collaborated), Remploy employed nearly 7,700 disabled people in eighty-seven factories – and the excess of expenditure over income was just over £5 million. By 1976–7, the last year for which figures are available, 7,972 disabled people were employed in the eighty-seven factories, at a cost of over £16 million. It is not a state secret, but neither has it been widely publicized that it would be cheaper if instead of going to work, all Remploy's disabled employees were to remain at home on social security. This was the conclusion reached by a departmental enquiry a few years ago.

The type of work undertaken has evolved over the years in a direction indicative of the problems which beset any non-commercial, work-providing enterprise, not excluding one as substantial as Remploy. In the early days, factories used to run several products on the one site, the idea being to accommodate different disabilities. With the multiplication of specialist staff and supervisors, and also of trade unions, Remploy headquarters became convinced this did not work, and work provision has been greatly simplified so that some factories concentrate on one type of product only.

The company consists of five trade groups, Engineering, Furniture, Knitwear, Leather and Textiles, and Packaging and Bookbinding; the balance between them, in terms of size and profitability, has varied with changing external industrial circumstances.

A major source of Remploy's work contracts is the priority suppliers scheme, the central contracting arrangement for placing government orders with institutions supported by public funds, Besides Remploy, these include prison industries, institutions for the blind, sheltered workshops for the disabled, and the Forces Help Society and Lord Roberts Workshops. Purchasing departments, such as the Post Office and the Ministry of Defence, and including the nationalized industries, are instructed to give priority suppliers the opportunity to manufacture the widest possible range of their requirements. The priority suppliers can obtain work either on a lowest tender basis or as a result of an offer on a fair price basis, the tenders being submitted on the basis of 'fit' labour costs, and the difference between 'fit' and 'disabled' productivity being met from the public purse. However, it has been indicated that the benefits of this rather cosy arrangement are about to be more widely dispersed to enable the smaller sheltered workshops, as well as Remploy and the Prison Industries, to participate more fully (*Developing Employment and Training Services for the Disabled*: para. 3.48).

In the matter of local contracts, Remploy has not been immune to competition from other sheltered workshops and, as the Consultative Document pointed out, it may be thought inappropriate that different categories of workshop, all Government funded, should be forced to scramble for work in this way. In Wales, for instance, Remploy and the Blind Workshops were at one time fighting each other quite hard for contracts. Hospital Industrial Therapy Units were also thought to be accepting work at unrealistic prices and undercutting sheltered workshops of every sort. In such a jungle, it is not surprising that Remploy, like other therapeutic workshops, has increasingly entered the field of sub-contracting for the final assemblers of the industries concerned.

*What Remploy does for the mentally ill* Our first contact with Remploy Personnel Department took place in 1967. It was already the policy not to accept a large concentration of mentally ill in one unit; where this was done, experience showed that the company could expect objections from supervisors and workers. The company therefore observes a working limitation of 10 per cent mentally ill throughout, though the proportion differs from factory to factory and at the time of our 1973 survey twenty-two works managers out of eighty-seven were employing none at all. Despite an overall increase in the Remploy category 'mental disorder', i.e. psychoneurosis and other mental illness and subnormality (1966: 13.6 per cent; 1971: 16.4 per cent; 1976: 20.2 per cent. *Remploy Personnel and Annual Statistics*), this limitation is still being observed, as the breakdown in *Table 3(2)* makes clear.

Table 3(2)    *Mental disorders 31 December 1976*

|  | males | females | all | % |
|---|---|---|---|---|
| psychoneuroses (e.g. anxiety or obsessional states, hysteria) | 267 | 79 | 346 | 4.4 |
| other mental illness (e.g. psychoses, schizophrenia, paranoia, dementia, psychopathic disorders) | 330 | 64 | 394 | 5.0 |
| mental sub-normality | 609 | 236 | 845 | 10.8 |
| total | 1,206 | 379 | 1,585 | 20.2 |

*Source: Remploy and Personnel Annual Statistics January 1977.*

Evidently, the overall increase must be attributed to a higher intake of the sub-normality category, since the mental illness categories still total only 9.4 per cent.

When in 1972 we embarked upon our first survey, Remploy works managers collaborated on a voluntary basis, to the extent of a 73 per cent response rate. Findings from this survey are discussed in later chapters, but it is worth mentioning in tribute to the quality of Remploy supervision that a higher proportion of skilled and semi-skilled psychiatrically disabled Remploy workers were found to be operating machines than the proportions of workers from the two open employment samples, yet Section II DPs work in Remploy because they are deemed incapable of work in open conditions.

One particular factory appeared from the correspondence to have an unusually large and successful ex-psychiatric patient element. We visited it to see why this was. We found that their selection process begins, as at all Remploys, with the DRO selecting from his register of severely disabled persons a number to attend for selection interview. If in any doubt about a person's potential, arrangements could be made at the adjoining Industrial Rehabilitation Unit for a short assessment or job rehearsal. In addition, new employees were on a three month's trial with fortnightly reviews of progress. Throughout, contact was maintained with everybody concerned. When ex-patients were first taken on, the works manager went to the hospital to be, as he said, 'indoctrinated'. Liaison with the consultant psychiatrist, still at the end of a telephone, was at first very close. The consultant and chief male nurse used to come to the factory every three weeks for consultations; about, for example, whether to put a patient on to a machine. The hospital social worker paid a weekly visit which the Remploy staff found of great value. He came with a supply of pills, but was also available to follow up any absence or problem. The DRO was always in touch. All this collaboration was now a matter of routine, and kept the wheels turning smoothly so that these Section II ex-patients were to be observed working on wood-cutting machines, veneer taping and glue spreading machines, as lipping press and drum sanding machine operators, press loaders, polishers, and inspectors. One ex-patient machine operator was now capable of setting his own machine: observing that the setter had them, this man went out and bought himself a ruler and set-square to do the job.

*How satisfactory has Remploy been for the mentally ill?*  The above factory is not typical, or the labour turnover statistics would not read as they do. By 1970 Remploy headquarters had become so disturbed by these that a statistical scrutiny was ordered. While of great interest, the analysis suffers from the fact that the category 'Mental and nervous disabilities' comprises not only mental illness and sub-normality, but epilepsy and organic conditions, brain damage, sciatica, cerebral palsy, and disseminated sclerosis, disorders so disparate as to severely limit its usefulness to us. We none the less learn the following.

The annual turnover rate for all disabilities in Remploy in 1970 stood at 18.1 per cent: 42 per cent of all leavers had less than one year's service, and 34 per cent less than six months' service. The breakdown by categories of disability showed that 37 per cent of all terminations occurred among the 'Mental and nervous disabilities' group (but since this group comprised 33½ per cent of the work force, the over-representation was not significant). However, half the leavers in this group were under 35 years of age; and turnover in their first two years of employment was 64 per cent compared with 50 per cent for the physically disabled groups.

Although Remploy management were disturbed at the training and administrative difficulties imposed by such a turnover, they none the less professed satisfaction at one aspect, namely the number who left sheltered work in Remploy for open industry. The figure quoted is 200 per annum, or 2–3 per cent. The Chairman in his annual review for 1970 remarked, 'Since its inception twenty-five years ago, we lost – and of this we are proud – 4,750 of our employees who left us to return to work in fit industrial occupations . . .' (*Remploy Annual Report* 1970). If these figures could be accepted unreservedly, no one would applaud them more than us, as champions of the rehabilitative component latent in sheltered work. But can they be so easily accepted?

In fact, just over 10 per cent of all terminations recorded by the 'Mental and nervous disabilities' group purported to be returns to open industry (Remploy 1970), but works managers suspected that an employee claiming to have found outside employment might be indulging in wishful thinking, or might even be hoping to fail so that he could return to the less pressurized certainty of unemployment and supplementary benefits. 'Such cases form a minority of the terminations but are sufficient to prevent any assumption that every return to open industry is a success story', commented the headquarters analyst.

These figures, despite the difficulties imposed by their non-comparability, have been taken apart to the best of our ability for this reason. Sheltered work for the severely mentally ill is widely viewed as a desideratum, almost a panacea, provision of which is sadly lacking and competition for which can be intense. But when ex-patients get it, what happens? They leave, in large numbers. For a very considerable number, it is plainly not the answer. Either they do indeed progress to open employment and a better wage, or for some the pressure is too great. To achieve the results reported of the factory visit, immense care was needed not only on the part of Remploy supervision but of hospital and community resources also. It is this array of liaison which seems to make sheltered work succeed.

### Croydon Local Authority

The London Borough of Croydon's Local Authority Rehabilitation and Assessment Centre (LARAC) provides an example of the second type of arrangement (*Figure 3(1)*).

Croydon's services for the disabled have been understandably adopted by both the health and employment ministries as their demonstration project, their showpiece. This has had its advantages and its disadvantages. The advantage has been that a fat injection of capital financing has come their way, such as a showpiece requires. The disadvantage has been that the resultant grandeur has had the effect of over-awing some of their visitors and would-be imitators, conscious that resources in their own, probably much smaller, areas would never be available for comparable developments. This is known to be the feeling of some of the DROs seconded for training courses in mental health before their own Leeds Training Centre was in operation.

The thing to do, therefore, when contemplating the largest of the London boroughs, is to attempt to disentangle from their peculiar advantages the principles and precepts which might be applied elsewhere.

First, what are the services, particularly the work provision services for the mentally disabled in Croydon? These can best be shown in one of the authority's own charts, given in *Figures 3(1)* and *3(2)* below.

Commenting from left to right, as it were, the referrals to the Crosfield Industrial Unit comprise mentally ill people, mentally handicapped, and physically handicapped, an integrated intake which is itself noteworthy. The bulk of mental illness referrals come from Warlingham Park Hospital, though the theoretical possibility of progress from day centres and day hospitals is not ruled out. The ratios of disability in 1978 stood at some 40 per cent mental illness, 40 per cent mental subnormality, and 20 per cent physical disability.

The composition of the Crosfield assessment panel, and of its complementary review panel, is of interest. The key is that both psychiatrist and clinical psychologist are holders of joint appointments from the health authority and the local authority: this dates back to the days of the late Dr A. R. May at Warlingham Park, followed by Dr J. W. D. Fisher, and of Dr S. L. Wright as Medical Officer of Health for the borough. In 1978, to take an example, the clinical psychologist at Warlingham Park was seconded for four days a week to the local

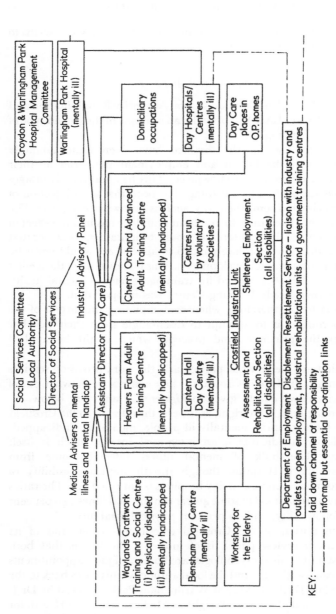

*Figure 3(1)* London Borough of Croydon/Croydon and Warlingham Park Hospital Management Committee
The Unified Industrial Work Service for the disabled
Basic structure and administration

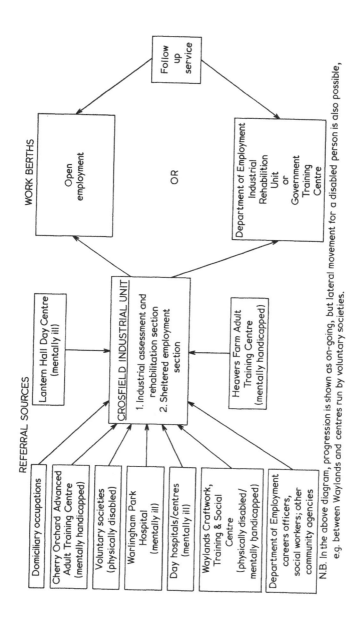

*Figure 3(2)* London Borough of Croydon/Department of Employment
The Unified Industrial Work Service
Rehabilitation possibilities for severely disabled persons

authority. The psychiatrists double the role of hospital consultant with that of local authority adviser in mental health and mental handicap. The arrangement is of course helped by the local authority and area health authority being coterminous.

Certain features relating to other personnel are also of interest. The successor to Mr K. G. Morley at the Crosfield Industrial Unit is an engineer by training. The Disablement Resettlement Officer who attends both panels is reinforced by a one-time colleague, a retired DRO who holds the local authority appointment of Placement Officer; it was found that the work was simply more than the official DRO service could cope with. Even so, it is felt that the unit could do with a social worker to sort out the numerous personal and benefit problems that arise; current policy, however, is to deploy social workers in area teams rather than to institutions where the work comes thickest.

Crosfield Industrial Unit itself stands at the centre of work provision. In administrative terms, it is double-barrelled. First, it is an approved Sheltered Workshop within the meaning of the Act, employing around 100 severely disabled people of all categories; and second, it contains an assessment and rehabilitation section, corresponding to an ITO, and giving intensive industrial training and preparation for open employment to around twenty trainees. When the Unit was established in this form in the late 1960s, it was considered that a concession had been wrung from the Department of Employment, who then still saw rehabilitation and sheltered work as two entirely separate entities. Since the Consultative Document on Sheltered Work, a milestone in this field, an arrangement such as this is applauded. Besides workers and trainees, a 'special group' has come into existence, consisting of recent trainees, mostly diagnosed mentally ill, who having spent the stipulated six months in the Assessment Unit would have had to be turned out unless retained in this group. In good times they might well have entered open employment. Even in 1977–8, and this is significant, many have been placed *after* the six month period allowable for rehabilitation and training grants.

Central to what might be termed the Croydon philosophy are the number and variety of out-working schemes based on Crosfield. Participants are both sheltered workers and rehabilitees sometimes working apart, sometimes together, an arrangement which does not appear to be upset by the difference between a training grant and the wage of a sheltered worker. In 1978, for example, there were three mobile work groups. One group looked after the gardens of old people on the Borough's estate. We saw another group concreting a driveway for a disabled tenant. A proposed painters' and decorators' group has run into union difficulties, which the disabled people's own shop steward appeared powerless, or unwilling, to help resolve. On a previous occasion the researcher heard of ex-patients placed in various domestic posts, and regularly visited by a psychiatric nurse trained Industrial Welfare Officer, peripatetically as in Bristol. But by no means all individual placements were domestic, and the work opportunities provided both by the authority and the hospital service could be with advantage noted elsewhere. Two clerical workers are employed in Croydon general hospitals. One ex-patient does micro-filming. One works in the Borough Valuer's office. Others are messengers.

The prototype local authority sheltered working group or enclave is at Holt Bros., manufacturers of motor car accessories, which already provides contracts to the Crosfield Unit. This group has been running continuously since 1970, except for one interruption at the time of the company's takeover. A group ranging from eight to twelve in number man a quite fast moving track on which are packaged, labelled, and packed a range of motor car accessories. Each time it was visited the group consisted in the main of mentally handicapped sheltered workers but there were also a few with a mental illness diagnosis, a spastic, and, in 1972, one or two severely physically disabled people. Over the years, a number of sheltered workers have been taken onto the Holts' pay-roll, as at Bristol. Over the years, the need to provide a special supervisor from Crosfield had declined and by 1978, the arrangement was that Holt Bros. should provide the supervision. The lady appointed had worked alongside the group for some time, but had no specific training, simply and successfully using her own common sense.

Considering all this, it must be asked how much of this thoughtful and well-directed provision could be duplicated elsewhere? Evidently the dovetailing of psychiatric theory and practice in hospital and community are of prime importance. The advantages of co-ordination and time-saving on the administrative side, and of continuity of care on the clinical side, made possible by joint appointments, are clear. The fact that the local authority and health authority areas are coterminous must help this process but is it essential for it? This is a most important question to which attention could be directed.

Another point. A tenet of faith held by Mr Ken Morley, who was so largely responsible for setting them up, is that all centres should be 'open-ended'. This too is crucial. From it follows the running together, in double harness, of sheltered work and rehabilitation. From it follows the mixed intake of referrals. From it follows the absence of artificiality that labelling can impose. Other features are the business-like yet sympathetic atmosphere prevailing at work; the appointment of an engineer; the back-up of orders and jobs provided by various departments of the borough; and the centralizing of contracts, the finding of which causes so many of the smaller workshops all over the country such difficulty.

A further, perhaps technical, point is the evidence that enclave arrangements must remain fluid and experimental, for even the special supervisor, thought to be the keynote of the enclave idea, has at Holt Bros. been dispensed with. In the present state of knowledge such flexibility is essential. Yet a further point is a clinical one, supplementing existing statistical series on rehabilitation outcome. This series is significantly age-related. Croydon Local Authority's first analysis, completed in 1971, showed that only 28 per cent of their ninety-two mentally ill people aged eighteen to thirty-nine entered open employment, compared with 62 per cent of the thirty-nine people in the forty to forty-nine age-group, a striking result indeed. The analyst comments: 'The reason for this is not apparent'. Must it not be that most of these subjects will have been diagnosed schizophrenic, with the younger of them still overtly or covertly ill, and the older of them, in the old terminology 'burnt-out'?

### Bristol ITO

Bristol ITO furnishes an example of an independent voluntary organization grant-aided by the Department.

For over twenty years Dr Donal Early, its founder, and the successive ventures which have sprung up in his wake have been in the forefront of each advance concerned with the rehabilitation for work of the mentally ill. A devoted clinician, he found it exhilarating to challenge the received Whitehall wisdom of the day on their behalf, and induce a change of attitudes. Following him came visitors from every continent, and the researchers amongst whom one of us is numbered.

The sequence began in the mid-1950s with industrial therapy at Glenside Hospital, Bristol. This was not the first unit. Premises and product were among the least promising, a dark and overcrowded redundant chapel in which the sole sub-contract, when the enterprise started, was for the assembly of ballpoint pens at the tightest of rates. What was unique was Dr Early's grasp of the immense potential of the new therapy. His capacity to enthuse not only his own staff and civic leaders but, crucially, imaginative industrialists such as Mr H. J. Dolman and Mr John Turley, ensured that the potential was exploited.

It soon became evident that industrial therapy units inside psychiatric hospitals stopped short of what was required if chronic long-stay patients were to be made fit for ordinary employment. The leap from hospital ward to shop floor was too great. And the government Industrial Rehabilitation Units and Training Centres dealt, as we have seen, with only a small number of cases (too small to discern any pattern in our samples), by means of short courses never intended for the slow progress of psychiatric patients.

An Industrial Therapy Organization is a registered company, limited by guarantee, non-profit making, and having a board of directors representative of church, civic, and industrial life. ITOs were set up specifically to rehabilitate, retrain by industrial methods and, where possible, resettle in open employment the long-stay mentally ill patient for whose needs the existing facilities of the Department of Employment had been shown to be inappropriate.

So in 1960 the first Industrial Therapy Organization was formed, ITO (Bristol) Ltd. ITO (Bristol) Ltd was soon followed by four others with identical articles of association: Epsom, Thames, Ulster, and Wirral. At the time of writing in 1978, only Thames survives, and this because at its inception its sponsors put up enough money to buy premises of which half could be let off to provide the organization with a continuing, dependable, cash flow. Of the others, Epsom ITO made a notable contribution over a span of ten years by demonstrating its trainees' ability to operate machines, and by insisting on the highest standards of personal turnout. Besides these, comparable organizations have sprung up outside the terms on which the Department of Employment insisted before grant-aiding, the most onerous being the limitation to a six-month period of training which could only in the most exceptional circumstances be extended to twelve months. Reading ITO, supported by a group of industrialists and first chaired by the local managing director of Courages Breweries, was one of those which preferred to retain its freedom of action. Another, Re-Instate Ltd, operated on the banks of the Thames at Erith in Kent, and, as so often, owed its existence to the determination of one dedicated individual, formerly an industrial chaplain. The Birmingham Industrial Therapy Association was something different again, more like a hospital industrial unit which happened to be sited outside, since its workers were paid only the therapeutic wage which, at the time of the research visit, was still under £2 per week if the worker were to remain eligible for social security benefits. The deadening effect of this earnings limitation, the real financial disincentive which it represented, had already become clear and we wrote about it extensively at the time (Wansbrough 1969). In Birmingham, however a certain motivation was provided because the Department of Employment set up an Industrial Rehabilitation Unit in the middle of the complex, and competition became keen to attain to the standard of the higher training allowances payable there.

The 1960 concept in Bristol was first for a contract workshop to which patients could progress from the rather restricted industrial units inside hospital, the hope being that after a period of time they would be fit for ordinary employment. But not all could make this grade, then or now. More sheltered employment was needed; for just as IRUs were inadequate for rehabilitation, so were Remploy and the thirty-seven local authority workshops inadequate, as regards places available, for sheltered work for the mentally ill. In fact, sheltered work provision is still inadequate, workshops being still in short supply and still difficult to maintain on a financially solvent basis. Perhaps the most persistent difficulty stems from the fact that the Department of Employment insists on identifying thirty potential workers before even contemplating a new unit. In consequence sheltered workshops have been in practice limited almost entirely to large centres of population, and as a curious result too, Dr Douglas Bennett's experimental workshop at the Maudsley Hospital cannot be supported by the Department of Employment but has had to look elsewhere for funding.

In Bristol further developments were afoot. By 1963 arrangements had been made for the first groups of ex-patients to work in local firms under sheltered work conditions. For this experiment the Department of Employment imposed certain conditions. ITO was to act throughout as the legal employer, paying all wages and taking out employers' liability insurance, ensuring that prospective workers were tried out in the ITO training factory for at least six months before proceeding outside, keeping their groups up to ten in number and arranging that they lived outside hospital. It was a great success, nevertheless. Labour was scarce, industry thriving. During those first years, the sheltered groups worked in four different factories, forty to forty-five at any given time, so that by 1970 no less than fifty-eight ex-patients could be counted as participating (retrospectively, for such was the heat of the battle that exact records were not kept until 1970). Pausing only to set up the Bristol Industrial Therapy Housing Association Ltd in 1965, Dr Early turned his attention once more to the Department of Employment, to point out the cramping effect of some of their conditions. For instance, few concerns were in a position to take on, let alone keep together in a group for supervisory purposes, as many as ten men. The Department therefore relaxed this condition, together with that requiring sheltered workers to work together under the direct supervision of a nurse. This crucially important officer was from May 1969 permitted to carry out his duties on a peripatetic basis, moving from factory to factory and individual to individual with the weekly wage packets and drug supply, thus imparting the touch of liaison and support which is one of the chief features of the scheme.

These are the bare historical bones. Amidst so much that is of importance in the history of the treatment of mental illness, one matter interests us particularly, that is the aspect of rehabilitation so vividly demonstrated as a possible element in some sheltered work.

### Rehabilitation in sheltered industrial groups – the enclave concept*

A year or so after the Department of Employment had relaxed the conditions described, one of us paid a visit to Bristol with the aim of scrutinizing the new sheltered work plan. By this date, 1970, the first four firms had been reduced to two. One firm had gone bankrupt, while in another the original group had dwindled to a handful largely because their ex-patients had been taken on to the pay-roll, i.e. had in effect been rehabilitated. The two schemes still operational offered an utter contrast. In one, a group of eleven women, employed in a long-established, paternalistic firm, behaved precisely as, at that time, the Disabled Persons' (Employment) Act expected them to behave – they appeared a compact, coherent, long-stay group, whom nobody expected to progress beyond their present status. This was by no means unenviable, for, like other women workers, they were earning the top rate for the district, qualifying for their pensions, bothering nobody, and being bothered by nobody. Situated thus, they had absolutely no incentive to press on to open conditions. No matter: this was a satisfactory outcome so far as it went.

But it may be thought that the second factory employing a sheltered working group had achieved even more, because many who had worked there had progressed to genuinely open conditions. At this factory, conditions were poor and the pay low. From here there was every incentive to move on, and from a group averaging ten or so at any one time no less than fourteen had done just this, to jobs in the co-op, the post office, on the buses, as van drivers, secretaries, labourers, and workers in paper making and cooked meat factories. To its credit, the

---

* These sheltered working groups, the creations of Dr Donal Early, were re-christened enclaves by the Department of Employment, and appeared as such for several years in official documents, notably the *Consultative Document on Sheltered Work* of 1973. Dr Early's insistence that 'a territory surrounded by foreign domination (OED)' was a scarcely appropriate rehabilitation milieu eventually prevailed, and the official (but not yet universally known) term is sheltered industrial groups.

Department of Employment drew the inescapable deductions from these Bristol experiments, and in the Consultative Document on Sheltered Employment advocated the Bristol policy of rehabilitation to outside employment by means of sheltered workshops, where possible employing enclaves or sheltered working groups (Wansbrough 1975).

Thus official recognition, acknowledgement, and even encouragement were bestowed, but by the time this occurred the economic climate in industry had imposed a standstill.

The figures in *Table 3(3)* illustrate a pinnacle of achievement in the years up to 1970, followed by the beginning of decline thereafter. The years 1975–7 have also seen no forward movement, and in the spring of 1978 Dr Early wrote (private communication) that he saw little sign of real improvement. Is this state of affairs due exclusively to industrial stagnation and high unemployment? To what extent can it be attributed to the 'wrong' candidates being referred from elsewhere, now that the backlog of chronic hospital cases has been gone through? Is work therapy (in its widest sense) of proven value only for the 'late' rehabilitation of the chronic schizophrenic? These are the current questions for debate.

Table 3(3)    *Outcome of Bristol sheltered industrial groups or enclaves 1963–74*

|  | 1963–70 | | 1970–74 | |
|---|---|---|---|---|
|  | *no.* | % | *no.* | % |
| to outside employment | 15 | 26 | 7 | 19 |
| still in group scheme | 12 | 21 | 19 | 53 |
| to ITO sheltered workshop | 3 | 5 | 3 | 8 |
| to ITO contract workshop | 6 | 10 | 4 | 11 |
| retired on pension | 7 | 12 | 1 | 3 |
| died | 3 | 5 | — | — |
| relapsed | 9 | 16 | 2 | 6 |
| not known | 3 | 5 | — | — |
|  | 58 | 100 | 36 | 100 |
|  | (male: 17 female: 41) | | (male: 24 female: 12) | |

*Note*: Moves to the ITO workshops are moves to less demanding situations.
*Source: Lancet* 21 June 1975

### The Peter Bedford Trust

Lastly, the Peter Bedford Trust is considered as an example of a quite independent body, making use of social security benefits, but without official sheltered work recognition and grant-aid.

Prominently displayed in the thoughtful literature put out by the Trust is a quotation from John Bellers (1654–1725), one of the first Quaker social campaigners and with Peter Bedford himself (1780–1864) one of its founding fathers. It reads:

'It is as much more charity to put the poor
in a way to live by their own work, than to
maintain them idle, as it would be to set
a man's broken leg, so that he might walk
himself, rather than always to carry him.'

The total argument of the Trust, and its methods, derive from Bellers. Those who are 'helped to self-help' are regarded not as patients, nor clients, but as participants in a joint venture which they contract to join. The central feature of the scheme is that accomodation is only offered after the contracting participants have demonstrated their desire to work and become independent. The contract which they sign embodying this commitment can be found in Appendix 1 (p. 183).

The Peter Bedford Project, the initial organization, was formed in 1969 as a committee of a Quaker foundation, the Bedford Institute Association, in order to test ways of resettling chronically unemployed, homeless, and rootless single people. It was the creation of Mr Michael Sorensen whose experience as a Senior Welfare Officer at Pentonville Prison, and as organizer of the Blackfriars Scheme for befriending ex-offenders, had led him to formulate specific ideas on the quite realistic terms on which such people could be helped. 'We ought to avoid "serving" people in a philanthropic way'. 'I came to think that befriending was more than the lonely man could stand. It was even . . . irrelevant to his needs, which had to do with counting for something in his own right . . . being seen to have something to give' (Sorensen 1968).

After a year or two's operation, it became necessary to form a Trust in order to secure separate charitable status. The project therefore is now divided into three separate legal entities, and their respective functions and overlapping membership need disentangling.

*The Peter Bedford Trust*, direct successor of the Peter Bedford Project, is now responsible for co-ordinating the work of all three bodies and for initiating experiments.

*The Peter Bedford Housing Association* was formed in 1971 to develop the accommodation offered to participants and to take advantage of the funding arrangements available to active housing associations. In its early years it was funded largely by the Joseph Rowntree Memorial Housing Trust, but the 1974 Housing Act made it possible for mainstream housing finance to be made available to bodies such as the Association and the bulk of funds now come from the Department of the Environment in the form of housing, not welfare, money. In its early years, too, the housing consisted of short-life properties, mainly in Islington, but a few in Hackney; and whereas there were advantages in this, notably of availability, the great disadvantage was the inherent insecurity operating on already insecure tenants. In 1975 the Association took over its first permanent property; by 1978 it had four with seven or eight others planned. With the prospect of some nice houses the Association feels in a position to initiate more constructive schemes, such as for instance, self-contained units for the occupation of tenants other than participants in order to avoid a ghetto-like situation developing. By 1978 the Association disposed of a total of thirty-five houses.

*John Bellers Ltd* provides employment opportunities. This orthodoxly structured, limited liability company, wholly owned by the Trust, took over the employment schemes already started by the Peter Bedford project in 1972 with a view to establishing them on a proper commercial basis. Their first Chairman, until he was appointed a Minister, was Mr David Ennals. Their first small trading profit was made in 1976. The appointment as general manager of Mr Roy Dady, who joined to take charge of the contract cleaning programme, was indicative of the professional and commercial approach, for he had held this responsibility in respect of London Airport.

The industrial and office cleaning work remains the core of the programme. Work is tendered for competitively, and has been principally won from the DHSS and the London Borough of Islington. The workforce usually numbers thirty or so, including a proportion, perhaps 30 per cent, of non-participants, to ensure the completion to a commercial standard of the contracts undertaken. The supervisors are mostly cleaning women, sympathetic but work-oriented. Between January 1974 and December 1975 the turnover on cleaning increased from £6,700 per annum to £61,700 per annum. A little building, decorating, and gardening, and a rather miscellaneous bundle · of activities euphemistically described as workshop training, complete the range of work on offer. The cleaning contracts are the base.

*Particulars of participants* The most recent count of particulars available was undertaken in 1975, when it was as shown in *Table 3(4)*.

Table 3(4) *Known social facts of those currently resident in Peter Bedford Housing Association (total no. of participants = 68)*

### residents' backgrounds

| | |
|---|---|
| in-patient psychiatric treatment | 40 |
| resident in sub-normality hospital | 8 |
| penal institution. | 7 |
| rootless (long-term use of reception centres) | 39 |
| treatment for alcoholism | 7 |
| acknowledged addiction to gambling | 3 |

(These figures represent the certain facts about participants and do not include any passing contact with institutions. Residents may appear in more than one category.)

### source of referral of current participants

| | |
|---|---|
| Probation service and prison | 2 |
| DHSS reception centres | 29 |
| subnormality hospital | 6 |
| psychiatric hospital | 17 |
| other voluntary agencies | 3 |
| social service department | 2 |
| self-referred | 9 |
| | 68 |

### age distribution of current participants

| | under 30 | 30–39 | 40–59 | 60 + |
|---|---|---|---|---|
| male | 5 | 10 | 32 | 6 |
| female | 1 | 2 | 8 | 4 |

### employment status of current participants

| | |
|---|---|
| employed full-time by John Bellers Ltd | 19 |
| full-time employment elsewhere | 19 |
| part-time employment by John Bellers Ltd or Peter Bedford Project, and on social security | 13 |
| old age pensioners | 4 |
| registered sick | 5 |
| supplementary or unemployment benefit | 7 |
| housewife | 1 |
| | 68 |

### reasons for leaving June 1969–December 1975

| | |
|---|---|
| alternative job/accommodation | 8 |
| entered psychiatric hospital | 9 |
| entered Camberwell Reception Centre | 8 |
| entered prison | 1 |
| given notice to quit because of arrears | 3 |
| not known | 11 |
| died | 7 |
| | 47 |

(N.B. 40 people who had taken up residence have left and not returned. Others have left and returned after absences of anything from a week to one year. The reasons given are only a concluding point of what may have been a long process in which many factors may feature. For example, no attempt has been made to establish for the purpose of this table why a man went back to the Camberwell Reception Centre.)

Visits to the Peter Bedford set-up and contact with the highly motivated staff have been much enjoyed. With the imaginative housing work we are not here concerned, beyond underlining that as researchers we agree that suitable housing for ex-patients is profoundly important, if not the *sine qua non* of successful resettlement in work. But it is of great significance that the Peter Bedford philosophy places work first and housing second, as a value judgement and in point of time. Accommodation offers are made after the handicapped person has demonstrated, by attempting to work, that he wishes to be responsible for himself. Other organizations will protest that they too share this philosophy but cannot lay hands on suitable work to be done. DHSS reception centres, workshops of all kinds, and in fact the old Poor Law Institutions themselves, share or shared this problem. This is where, again, the John Bellers set-up has so much to commend it since it offers unpressured employment, in the company of some ordinary workers, for full-time or varied part-time hours according to the health and strength of the re-emerging worker. The experiment of using contract cleaning as the vehicle for this requirement has now been in progress for nearly ten years, and can be regarded as of proven value. It is known that the Manpower Services Commission has been asked by the National Advisory Council for the Employment of Disabled People to explore the possibility of government central contracts being placed in the way of smaller sheltered workshops, besides Remploy. Perhaps government contracts for services such as cleaning could also be eased in the direction of organizations such as John Bellers Ltd?

### Comment

Shortcomings in the state services for the mentally ill stem, as we have seen, from attempts to slot them into fast throughput schemes on the physical model and, when they appeared too numerous, refusing to accept them altogether. If no blame attaches to the Department of Employment in the early years, the same cannot be said after the departmental committee of 1964 and the Tunbridge Committee had reported. The situation therefore now is that the quota scheme has fallen into disarray while mentally ill people still fit uneasily into ERC and Remploy strategies. But whereas the ERC is reviewing its methods, Remploy gives little evidence of progress in service towards mentally ill people. The figure that sticks in the mind is that on a census date in April 1972, twenty-two out of sixty-seven Remploy Works Manager respondents had no mentally ill people on their books at all. Yet Remploy receives by far the major share of the sheltered work vote.

The thinking of those in charge of state services left a gap into which stepped the ITO movement (for it is in the quality of its thinking rather than the eventual scale of what was intended to be a national movement that its importance lies). Croydon drove home the same lessons from a local authority standpoint. The lessons were: first, the need for lengthy rehabilitation; second, the advantage of an open ended set-up which is simply not paralleled in the field of physical disability, so that assessment, rehabilitation, and sheltered work can proceed together without artificial administrative barriers. This point requires elaboration. It has been emphasized that for some mentally ill people (but of course not all) only arrangements made under sheltered work auspices offer long enough periods for rehabilitation. That is to say, the distinction between rehabilitation and sheltered work is for them artificial, and does not correspond to their requirements. In the same way, assessment of employability (despite valiant attempts to devise criteria on the part of Bennett, Watts, and Griffiths) cannot yet generally be made away from the work situation – sheltered or open. We were constantly told in the course of visits that even the most experienced clinicians could not make these predictions. You need workplace pressure to give the authentic atmosphere, though the various rehearsals like clock cards, lengthening hours and so on, help. Croydon believes strongly in running all three functions together; assessment, rehabilitation, and sheltered work. So did Bristol, complaining vigorously because the six months assessment period demanded by the Department before they would grant aid sheltered work was not also funded from central sources.

Is not some device to ensure this trinity of operations one of the great needs? Is it perhaps hindered by administrative divisions at the centre? We can recall once discussing a similar issue with a Department of Employment spokesman, to be confronted by the official line distinguishing (incontrovertibly) between matters of health and matters of employment, with a department of state responsible for each. We can remember his amazement on hearing of the existence of the working-out patient, that illogical hybrid, a full-time hospital patient who is simultaneously a full-time worker in open employment. But this horror of administrative untidiness remains the best solution for some patients now as then.

The third point is not so much a lesson as an issue raised. Croydon's joint appointments of personnel to local and health authorities are of evident benefit, administratively and clinically (as they have been in Nottinghamshire). The coterminous boundaries of the two authorities must have facilitated arrangements, but one wonders if these are essential. If boundaries are not coterminous, and, for example, a hospital covers a number of local authorities, could not a consultant be appointed to the one responsible for its largest catchment area? If a large authority has within its boundaries more than one hospital, could these not agree on a representative so that the psychiatric hospital viewpoint would not go by default where a fusing of objectives, rather than a passing of bucks, is the paramount need. Already the community psychiatric nursing service has been installed in one vaccum: joint funding in another. Perhaps joint appointments should as a matter of policy be more actively sought, particularly should there be available a specialist in rehabilitation as recommended by Tunbridge, or a clinical psychologist similarly interested.

# 4

## Design of the research programme

### Introduction

In Chapter 2 we identified and estimated the approximate size of the former in-patient population in employment, and Chapter 3 examined the current provision designed for the support of this group. These were the preliminaries to our main objective, which is to look in more detail at the characteristics of this population. There are many methodological problems involved in the design of such an investigation. We will consider some of them and describe the series of studies undertaken, which were designed to illuminate different facets of the overall problem.

### The existence of an ideal sample frame?

There is no way in which all former psychiatric hospital in-patients in employment can be delineated from the population at large. No definitive listing of such people exists. We do however know that the proportion of the working-age population at large falling into this sub-group is small – about 5 per cent. It would thus require a very large sample of the working population in order to sift a substantially sized sample of former in-patients. The stigma attached to mental illness means that many conceal it, and those sifted would be unlikely to represent a random sample from the study population. Thus, this method of generating a sample from the unlisted frame of all former in-patients would be unlikely to be successful.

A possible approach to a frame of employees is through employers. In theory each employer has a list of all his employees, and the frame of employers may be regarded as providing a latent frame for employees.

Frames of employers are not readily available. There exists a national frame derived for taxation purposes which lists all PAYE points. In many cases an employer will have more than one PAYE, point, e.g. for works and staff employees separately, and thus the frame will contain duplicates. There are confidentiality problems surrounding the frame, and whilst access to its summary characteristics is possible, a sample of individual employers with addresses is not readily accessible. Even if it were, it would be less than ideal for our purposes. It is unlikely that an employer with several PAYE points will divide medical and personnel records into similar groups at the same locations. Thus an enquiry addressed to a PAYE point would not gain access to employee listings with identifying information useful to our purpose.

Local Department of Employment offices (job centres) maintain registers of employers. Until approximately 1974 the register at each local office was kept in a standard form. More recently the form of each register has been largely at the discretion of local management. In the majority of cases the register only contains employers who have used the job centre services, so that many firms who recruit directly or via commercial agencies will be omitted. There is no system whereby employers are deleted from the list if they cease trading, thus the list can contain many 'blanks'. Despite these unsatisfactory features this sample frame has been used in several studies. Compared to the distribution of the firms in the national frame it has been found to be particularly deficient in employers with a small number of employees (Goddard 1976). For our purposes the frame is more satisfactory than the national listing as it gives access to those responsible for personnel matters in each company, who in turn will have access to employee records which may enable former in-patients to be identified for sampling purposes.

Even if we regard this locally based sample frame of employers as satisfactory and assume that employers will be able to identify former in-patients easily from their records, the collection of detailed inform-ation about individual employees presents difficulties. Although we deal with employers and do not seek direct responses from employees, much of the information collected will have been given in confidence by the employee upon engagement and thus it is axiomatic that the employee's agreement to participation in the study should be obtained. In many cases employers would feel that some consultation with and agreement from local trade union officials would be necessary before taking part in the study. Amongst the majority of employers there is little awareness of occupational health beyond the usual hazard provisions, thus in some companies finding a motivated, skilled, and reliable respondent would not be straightforward. These difficulties are inter-linked as an employer aware of the wider context of occupational health is usually keen to participate in any study and able to provide a reliable respondent. The atmosphere which pervades such companies usually ensures a workforce who are prepared to participate and not suspicious of the motives for the data collection.

The studies undertaken used specialized frames with a more limited coverage than these two frames described. These specialized frames homed in upon firms with an awareness of occupational mental health and an availability of reliable record keepers. Thus the quality of the data was good and the costs of its collection kept low.

In order to set these studies into the national context, a postal inquiry with a sample from the locally based national frame was also undertaken. This obtained simple information on employers and their employment policies in the field of mental health.

## The design and sampling biases of the three major investigations

### Sample B

A latent frame exists within each of those hospitals which maintain formal or informal contacts with local employers for the purpose of placing former patients in employment. Not every hospital follows this practice and in many hospitals that do the contacts are through an individual nurse or social worker rather than a formal relationship between employer and hospital. Part of this latent frame was realized by writing to all psychiatric hospitals in England and Wales having over 100 beds and asking if they maintained such contacts with employers, and if they would make a list of them available as part of a sample frame for the enquiry.

245 employers' names were received from forty-four hospitals; twenty-five employers took part in a pilot study. Each employer was asked to provide details of occupational health arrangements in regard to mental health and information about his experience of employing the formerly mentally ill. In addition employers were asked to provide details about former in-patient employees. Employees were divided into two groups: 'new' employees, i.e. those who had not previously been engaged by the employer, and 'old' employees, i.e. those who prior to their recent spell in hospital had been working for the employer. These employees' details were collected retrospectively for up to six employees in each category. The period of enquiry was limited to the three years preceding the survey date and in the event that more than

Table 4(1)  *Geographical Structure of Hospital-based Sample(B)*

| hospital region | hospitals | | employers | | | employees | |
|---|---|---|---|---|---|---|---|
| | population | sample | listed by hospitals | co-operated | provided employee data | 'old' | 'new' |
| Newcastle Region | 8 | 1 | 2 | 2 | 1 | 1 | 0 |
| Leeds Region | 11 | 2 | 10 | 3 | 3 | 0 | 6 |
| Sheffield Region | 11 | 1 | 5 | 4 | 4 | 1 | 7 |
| East Anglian Region | 7 | 3 | 11 | 6 | 5 | 0 | 10 |
| North West Metropolitan Region | 6 | 4 | 39 | 17 | 10 | 5 | 30 |
| North East Metropolitan Region | 5 | 3 | 17 | 8 | 4 | 0 | 14 |
| South East Metropolitan Region | 9 | 4 | 9 | 6 | 5 | 7 | 16 |
| South West Metropolitan Region | 13 | 6 | 39 | 25 | 22 | 12 | 84 |
| Wessex Region | 7 | 3 | 39 | 20 | 15 | 10 | 39 |
| Oxford Region | 6 | 2 | 17 | 11 | 7 | 5 | 13 |
| South Western Region | 10 | 2 | 6 | 4 | 3 | 0 | 4 |
| Welsh Region | 10 | 3 | 6 | 4 | 1 | 0 | 2 |
| Birmingham Region | 11 | 8 | 28 | 14 | 8 | 12 | 14 |
| Manchester Region | 5 | 2 | 17 | 6 | 3 | 1 | 3 |
| Liverpool Region | 3 | 0 | 0 | 0 | 0 | 0 | 0 |
| England & Wales | 122 | 44 | 245 | 130 | 91 | 54 | 242 |

*Source:* Wansbrough and Cooper 1978

six employees were eligible, details of the six hired most recently were requested. This sample of 'hospital-liaising' employers is referred to as Sample B.

Many hospitals did not maintain regular contacts with employers, but relied for job placement on the statutory agencies; others declined to provide the addresses of employers lest this should prejudice the relationships they had built up.

The distribution of employers and employees is shown in *Table (1)*. Whilst neither the sample of employers nor the sample of employees can be regarded as random, most regions are adequately represented. The bias is towards the metropolitan regions – 47 per cent of employers, 44 per cent of 'old' employees, and 59 per cent of 'new' employees were from these areas. Compared to the distributions of employers in England and Wales by size and industry type, our sample contains a disproportionate number of large industrial employers and is lacking in smaller employers from the 'service' industries (*Tables 4(2)* and *4(3)*).

## Sample C

Another latent frame exists through the agency of occupational health doctors. The majority of physicians with an interest in occupational

Table 4(2) *Percentage distribution by Registrar General's Classification of all employers and those providing employee details for each sample compared with Census of Employment distribution for England and Wales 1975*

| Classification | sample B | | sample C | | England and Wales 1975 % |
| | all % | providing employee details % | all % | providing employee details % | |
| --- | --- | --- | --- | --- | --- |
| industry | 59.2 | 57.1 | 77.7 | 80.8 | 20.9 |
| agriculture & horticulture | 0.8 | 1.1 | 0 | 0 | 0.1 |
| professional, scientific & commercial | 3.1 | 4.4 | 4.7 | 6.1 | 15.2 |
| distributive trades & services | 23.1 | 25.3 | 12.1 | 7.1 | 56.9 |
| public administration & defence | 13.8 | 12.1 | 5.4 | 5.1 | 6.9 |
| no. of employers | 130 | 91 | 148 | 99 | 917,297 |

*Source*: Wansbrough and Cooper 1978

Table 4(3)   *Percentage distribution by size of work force of all employers and those providing employee details for each sample compared with Census of Employment distribution for England and Wales 1975*

| size of workforce | sample B | | sample C | | England and Wales 1975 % |
| --- | --- | --- | --- | --- | --- |
| | all % | providing employee details % | all % | providing employee details % | |
| 0–9 | 6.2 | 5.5 | 0.7 | 0 | 70.1 |
| 10–24 | 6.9 | 8.8 | 0 | 0 | 16.7 |
| 25–49 | 12.3 | 9.9 | 0 | 0 | 6.5 |
| 50–99 | 16.9 | 16.5 | 0.7 | 1.0 | 3.3 |
| 100–199 | 15.4 | 16.5 | 0.7 | 0 | 1.8 |
| 200–499 | 18.5 | 17.6 | 4.1 | 4.0 | 1.1 |
| 500+ | 23.8 | 25.3 | 93.9 | 95.0 | 0.5 |
| no. of employers | 130 | 91 | 148 | 99 | 917,297 |

*Source*: Wansbrough and Cooper 1978

health belong to the Society of Occupational Medicine (SOM), although not all such doctors are employed as 'industrial' medical officers, nor do they all maintain an interest in mental health. The Society of Occupational Medicine agreed to make available its list of 884 UK based members. The primary units of the SOM sample were the 226 members of the Society who had indicated both an interest in the research topic and a willingness to provide information about ex-patient employees.

Soon after the Sample B investigation, a similar enquiry was conducted through this sample. The fact that the respondents were medical officers allowed some direct questions to be asked about employees' medical history, which could not be put to Sample B employers: apart from this, the enquiry took the same form as that for Sample B. Positive response was obtained from 148 respondents (65 per cent) and schedules of ex-patient employees were provided by ninety-nine organizations (44 per cent). This sample of SOM members is referred to as Sample C. The overt biases of the sample, compared to the distributions for England and Wales, are towards employers in large scale industrial manufacturing (*Tables 4(2)* and *4(3)*).

Both these investigations were retrospective, and the enquiries about experiences with individual employees were of a very general kind. The objective was to identify successful matches of ex-patient employee to employer and job, and to isolate problems which were experienced by the majority of employers. In the event, sickness absence and certain aspects of performance and behaviour were seen as the concerns of employers and many indications of other patterns were identified, e.g. an apparent problem with non-manual work.

### Sample D

A careful evaluation of sickness absence and work behaviour patterns necessitated a prospective study with a regular series of enquiries over an extended period. Thus the importance of keen, well motivated and reliable respondents was even more vital than for the two earlier studies. This and the fact that we saw the need to make extensive enquiries about employees' hospital records indicated that another sample obtained via the SOM-based latent frame was most appropriate.

When in 1972 the SOM membership had been circularized with an invitation to take part in the C Study, they were asked to indicate a willingness or the reverse to participate in the record-keeping study should this take place. When the D Study was authorized, an updated SOM membership list was utilized to ensure that all current members had been invited to participate. The total number of doctors from both lists who expressed a preliminary interest in the D Study was 499.

The number of actual respondents (as opposed to firms) was fifty-two: one respondent in an industrial health service provided information in respect of employees in seven firms, making a total of fifty-nine separate employers. Every effort was made to encourage employers to attempt to list all ex-patient employees (in part or all of the workforce) and to select randomly from this list. In records not flagged for this purpose this presented an unacceptable task, and in the event some two-thirds of the subjects were selected by using the knowledge of medical staff and the remainder by random selection from part or all of the workforce.

Nine respondents searched all their records and found forty eligible subjects of whom twenty-six were chosen; four of these refused to take part leaving a realized sample of twenty-two subjects. Eight respondents searched some section of their records, finding over fifty eligible subjects of whom forty-three were invited to participate; five of these refused leaving a realized sample of thirty-eight subjects. Thus sixty subjects were obtained from this sampling procedure. Thirty-five respondents searched no records at all, but from personal knowledge were able to list over 370 eligible subjects. Of these 128 were chosen, eight of these refused, leaving a realized sample of 120. The total realized sample of 180 was well spread across respondents with sixteen providing records of only one subject, thirteen entering two subjects, nineteen entering three to eight subjects, and only four entering ten or more subjects. Only 16 per cent of the sample were recognized as having a psychiatric history at the time they were taken on, the discovery being made subsequently for 80 per cent. The sample is therefore mainly made up of long service employees who are, however, not necessarily a long time out of hospital. This second SOM based sample is referred to as Sample D.

Table 4(4)   *Second sample of SOM members*

| | |
|---|---:|
| total numbers of doctors on our lists | 449 |
| number falling outside the scope of the study: | |
| not contacted for specific reason | 8 |
| no success in contacting, died, etc. | 15 |
| no clinical responsibility | 71 |
| doctor or nurse leaving or left, off sick, or away | 16 |
| no employee eligible | 25 |
| | 135 |
| personal contact never established | 18 |
| contacted but no decision received (i.e. refusal by implication) | 79 |
| number declining to participate: | |
| too busy, understaffed, staff problems, collection of data too difficult, etc. | 65 |
| actual or potential union or management opposition | 14 |
| study considered to be potentially harmful to employees | 15 |
| other reason | 22 |
| no reason stated | 26 |
| | 142 |
| number to whom questionnaires despatched | 71 |
| number of subsequent withdrawals | 12 |
| size of sample | 59 |

For Study D we collected little information about the fifty-nine employers involved. Many of the participating doctors (though not the employees) were the same as in Study C and the overt bias of the sample towards large firms in manufacturing industry is the same as that demonstrated for Study C ( *Tables 4(2)* and *4(3)*).

The sample of employees obtained in Study D was examined for its overt biases in view of the *ad hoc* methods adopted for the sampling of ex-patient employees within firms. *Table 4(5)* displays the important features of this analysis. The selected subjects tend to be slightly younger and probably as a consequence have spent slightly less cumulative time in hospital than those who were randomly chosen. Those selected have a slightly higher average number of previous hospital admissions and a markedly lower time in months since last discharge – an average of twenty-eight months for those selected compared to sixty-seven months for those chosen at random. This is not surprising as it will be those more recently out of hospital who come immediately to the minds of the firms' doctors. However it results in this group being perhaps less well recovered than the randomly chosen group.

Table 4(5)    *Basic characteristics of subjects of Study D by method of selection from employer records*

| determinants of sample | selected subjects (120) | randomly choosen subjects (60) |
|---|---|---|
| number of previous hospital admissions | 2.3 | 1.7 |
| previous cumulative stay in hospital (weeks) | 23.9 | 27.6 |
| months since last hospital discharge (at beginning of study) | 28.1 | 67.4 |
| age in years at beginning of study | 43.3 | 46.3 |

## The biases inherent in the sampling frame of doctors

In the attempt to obtain a sample of all former in-patients in employment in England and Wales, Study D comes nearest to the ideal: the sampling biases inherent in this study have already been described.

However, the original frame of occupational health doctors does not, evidently, provide complete coverage of the whole population and this under-coverage in turn introduces bias. It is worth considering for a moment whether alternative strategies might have yielded greater advantages, (although the approach to employers was decided upon at an early stage for reasons other than statistical).

The quite common method of following a discharge cohort from a hospital would overcome under-coverage but has other drawbacks. There is a confidentiality issue in the use of medical records to gain access to subjects; and to be a practical proposition the investigation must be confined to a small number of hospitals. If an idea of the effect of 'time since discharge' on employment prospects is to be obtained then the sample must be drawn from several annual discharge cohorts. This can compound one of the major problems inherent in a study of this kind, that of locating subjects. The older the discharge record the more unlikely it is that the subject can be contacted by this means. Easily located subjects themselves form a biased sample, e.g. those with family ties, with the result that the realized sample would be likely to have as many imperfections as our own achieved through employers. However, immediacy of contact with ex-patients possesses its own value, and the plan for the whole research included a study of a discharge cohort for one year, some results from which are included in our discussions (Shea 1978). In the event, of course, we were fortunate to be granted the collaboration of occupational health doctors and we now indicate how these are distributed, and with what consequences for the representativeness of our realized sample.

*Table 4(6)* sets out the estimated provision of occupational health personnel among employers in England and Wales. Full- or part-time professional staff are confined to a small percentage of employers, but they are the employers of large workforces. Thus over 60 per cent of the national workforce is covered by one of the types of provision outlined in *Table 4(6)*. Provision also varies across different industrial groups, being highest in the 'hazard' areas of heavy industry and lowest in the service industries. The size distribution of employers' firms in each industrial grouping reinforces this effect. In summary: our approach through the sampling frame of occupational health doctors offers access to a further

Table 4(6)   *Provision of occupational health personnel among employers in England and Wales*

| category of personnel | % of all firms having this provision |
|---|---|
| full-time doctor on site | 0.6 |
| part-time doctor on site | 6.0 |
| full-time nurse on site | 4.9 |
| part-time nurse on site | 2.7 |
| doctor's services retained and used as required | 18.6 |
| doctor available at another site e.g. headquarters | 9.2 |

*Note*: The percentages are not cumulative. A single employer may have more than one category of personnel.

frame consisting of some 60 per cent of all employees (though not necessarily 60 per cent of all eligible former in-patients); the coverage will be better in the manufacturing than in the service industries.

At the second stage of sampling, which is sampling within the occupational health doctors' firms, other problems of bias will arise.

It is by no means certain that an employer will know all his employees who have been psychiatric in-patients. We have already noted the probability that he will know most of those whose initial in-patient spell has occurred during their current employment, but that a probably quite large proportion of those hospitalized prior to their engagement by him will not be known to him as former in-patients. This state of affairs will have resulted from a policy that requires a job applicant, answering a screening questionnaire, to respond to a question about any previous history of 'nervous or mental troubles'. It is common practice amongst the symptom-free, less overtly ill to conceal any such history. *Table 4(7)* indicates that the presence of professional staff, which is closely correlated with the size of the workforce, is associated with an increased use of pre-engagement medical examinations or screening health questionnaires. This phenomenon could result in a large number of the less overtly ill members of our sample frame being excluded from this second stage sampling, simply because they are unknown to their employers. It is also reasonable to suspect that the occupational health doctors' frame (for Samples C and D) may have excluded honest, symptom-free individuals who have been refused employment on the basis of their responses to health questionnaires.

Table 4(7)   *Occupational health policy on engagement of employees: percentages of employers within occupational health provision categories*

| occupational health policy | occupational health provision | | | |
| --- | --- | --- | --- | --- |
| | *full-time doctor* | *part-time doctor* | *full-time nurse* | *all employers* |
| medical examination for: | | | | |
| all employees | 30 | 16 | 19 | 8 |
| certain grades only | 70 | 54 | 41 | 27 |
| no employees | 0 | 30 | 40 | 65 |
| health questionnaire for: | | | | |
| all employees | 39 | 47 | 51 | 27 |
| certain grades only | 61 | 14 | 26 | 9 |
| no employees | 0 | 39 | 23 | 64 |

In absolute figures, the extent of the under-coverage of our latent frame can only be given imprecisely. Study C and Study D indicate that roughly one in 150 to one in 200 of the workforce will be known to an employer as former in-patients. Thus the potential size of the latent frame is about 65,000 to 85,000. The number of former in-patients in employment, or seeking it, we have estimated in Chapter 2 as some 700,000. It follows that the frame's coverage is of about 10–15 per cent of all eligible employees. The biases inherent in this under-coverage tend towards the overtly ill, in large firms having an occupational health department.

## The specialized studies

The major studies described, based on open employment Samples B, C, and D were preceded and accompanied by several special investigations, to which reference will also be found in the following pages.

(a) Resettlement schemes in open industry. The whole research programme commenced in 1970 with a review of the schemes already existing in industry for the resettlement of former patients. Some of these had been identified in the course of earlier research on the industrial therapy movement but, in the event, further search showed them to be so scarce on the ground as hardly to affect the total problem, except as trail-blazers, in which respect their contribution is indeed notable.

Rehabilitation and sheltered work, administered through no less than eight distinct methods, were reviewed in Industrial Therapy Organizations both grant-aided and independent, and in schemes found in Basingstoke, Middlesex, Scunthorpe, Sheffield, and the motor industry. The purpose of this preliminary study was to describe and evaluate these, so that good practice, sheer ingenuity, and practical know-how might be more widely disseminated. This is the 'Interim Report' of our text.

(b) Remploy. The Remploy organization is the major sheltered employer of disabled people, its remit covering the mentally as well as the physically disabled. As a sample frame, it offered the certainty of at least some psychiatric cases, and it was thought that an examination of their experiences would be valuable in itself and for purposes of comparison. Some sixty-four Remploy works managers provided information akin to that provided by the hospital-liaising employers in Sample B. Schedules of forty-five 'old' employees and 142 'new' employees were obtained. This sample is referred to as Sample A.

(c) The case studies. Meanwhile it had been realized that prospectively obtained information would offer substantial advantages over the retrospective data already received, particularly for the minute investigation of sickness absence and relapse. But doubts were expressed as to the feasibility of setting up the necessary contemporaneous recording, both on grounds of practicality and of confidentiality. Three case studies were therefore established in three manufacturing companies whose occupational health staff proffered their services for this purpose. It was found possible and acceptable to keep records for a year and as a result of these piloting exercises, Study D was embarked upon.

(d) Sickness absence. One subsidiary study concentrated on the excessive sickness absence identified as a major concern amongst employers. With the co-operation of a large employer in manufacturing industry we obtained access to certified sickness absence records over the period 1966–74 for three samples of male employees. The samples consisted of fifty-four former in-patients, seventy-one employees with a history of coronary disease, and a sample of ninety-two employees chosen from the workforce at large. These data allowed the characteristics of the absence patterns of the groups to be compared and contrasted.

Each of these four studies focuses on different aspects. In them we make no attempt to draw inferences to the whole employment field, but merely to document and illuminate facets of the problem which had been highlighted before and during the major investigations.

(e) Occupational health facilities in England and Wales. A postal enquiry using lists of employers at employment exchanges was conducted with a view to assessing the biases inherent in the SOM sampling frame. Results from this study are used in *Tables 4(6)* and *4(7)*.

## Diagnosis

Our method of data collection at second hand, and, indeed, the inherent difficulties surrounding the concept of diagnosis in mental illness, make us hesitant to be categorical on this subject. Nevertheless we believe it right to set out a remarkable congruence of percentage distributions of diagnosis observed in our samples. The data derive from Samples C and D, plus a large manufacturing company represented by Case Study A. Though this latter sample totals only thirty-one, we shall quote it in percentage form to point up the striking similarity.

Table 4(8)    *Diagnosis: Percentage distribution of ex-patient employees in four samples*

| diagnosis | Case Study A 1973 no. = 31 % | Sample C 1974 (i) no. = 396 % | (ii) no. = 138 % | Sample D 1977 no. = 180 % |
|---|---|---|---|---|
| psychoses | 19 | 18 | 20 | 18 |
| depressions | 58 | 58 | 42 | 59 |
| neuroses | 16 | 14 | 17 | 19 |
| personality disorders | 3 | 2 | 7 | 2 |
| alcoholism and addiction | 3 | 6 | 9 | 2 |
| other, the residual category comprising disorders of organic origin, subnormality, epilepsy, etc. | 0 | 2 | 5 | 0 |

It thus appears that, of all known subjects now working in large-scale industry, nearly one in five is likely to have been psychotic; and since in the above table all forms of depression have been classified together, psychosis is here almost synonymous with schizophrenia.

## Inferences from the investigation

For convenience of reference, the numbers involved in the questionnaire-based studies are listed below:

| sample respondents | old employees | new employees |
|---|---|---|
| A: 42 Remploy managers | 45 | 142 |
| B: 92 concerned employers | 54 | 242 |
| C: 92 occupational health doctors | 405 | 148 |
| D: 59 occupational health doctors | 180 | |
| Total of over 240 respondents (some doctors participated in both C and D Studies) | Total of 1216 subjects | |

But we must reiterate the point made in our introduction to this chapter. The series of studies is designed to cast light upon different aspects of the whole population and no one study is capable of providing inferences to the whole. Each study should be seen in its context and any inferences drawn should be wholly within this context.

# 5

# Work and the working environment

## Types of occupation

Since it became clear that psychiatrically disturbed people could be resettled in work if indeed they were not already there, successive ideas, theories, or perhaps myths have been propounded as to the type of work they could do, and more particularly, not do. Setting up our three empirical studies, we held discussions with a wide range of employers and occupational health doctors who all fed us impressive reasons why their particular industry offered an unsuitable milieu. Seafaring meant the presence of cheap and plentiful liquor and the absence of skilled medical help. Working with dangerous substances was self-evidently unthinkable. Hazardous conditions and small group interdependence ruled out coal-mining. Chemists' shops offered access to drugs and other service industries involved face to face contact with the public. These prohibitions, at first faithfully noted, were soon realized to be drawing the net wider than need be. What about shipping company employees who never go to sea? Or surface workers at the pits? Records were then received for our D Study relating to employees in some of the most dangerous industries, which cannot be named because of the outcry that would result, and the wrong alarmist conclusions that would be drawn. As an industrial medical officer in one of the most hazardous industries remarked in correspondence: in a given industry not all the jobs will be dangerous; some will be suitable, others not.

Ideally it should be possible to specify which these are, and often in a rough and ready way this is done; jobs such as storeman, messenger, or the servicing of an assembly line are kept for a firm's own walking wounded, including people with a psychiatric history, or for point of retirement employees needing an easier job after perhaps years on a fast track. On a research visit some years ago, the chief medical officer of a large manufacturing company joked about their central stores. Whenever he went there he was greeted by numerous old friends, now storekeepers; indeed he had to refrain from suggesting this destination for more ex-patients, lest, so to speak, the blind were reduced to leading the blind. To go further than this, however, and attempt to compile a checklist of all suitable jobs, would be impossible on the data available even were it thought useful. Instead we have classified the occupations of all ex-patients entered in our studies according to accepted schemes, and the resultant descriptive information is, we believe, in itself of value, since it demonstrates what jobs are currently held by ex-patients. It also provides material by which crudely to estimate how successfully these jobs are being done, and by which to assess also the validity of some of the theories on the suitability of different occupations which have held sway.

Table 5(1)   *Occupations of members of Samples B and C*

| | Sample B | | | | Sample C | | | |
|---|---|---|---|---|---|---|---|---|
| | I old | II new | total | % | I old | II new | total | % |
| 1 managers and professions | 4 | 1 | 5 | 1.7 | 46 | 2 | 48 | 8.7 |
| 2 intermediate, supervisory, technical | 4 | 3 | 7 | 2.4 | 44 | 6 | 50 | 9.0 |
| 3 clerical | 9 | 15 | 25 | 8.4 | 58 | 34 | 92 | 16.7 |
| 4 personal and catering | 3 | 34 | 37 | 12.5 | 5 | 6 | 11 | 2.0 |
| 5 skilled manual machine | 2 | 5 | 7 | 2.4 | 28 | 5 | 33 | 6.0 |
| 6 skilled manual non-machine | 2 | 5 | 7 | 2.4 | 45 | 12 | 57 | 10.3 |
| 7 semi-skilled manual-machine | 5 | 12 | 17 | 5.7 | 36 | 7 | 43 | 7.8 |
| 8 semi-skilled manual non-machine | 19 | 82 | 101 | 34.1 | 96 | 42 | 138 | 25.0 |
| 9 unskilled | 5 | 83 | 88 | 29.7 | 46 | 30 | 76 | 13.8 |
| 10 not known | 1 | 1 | 2 | 0.7 | 3 | 1 | 4 | 0.7 |
| | 54 | 242 | 296 | 100.0 | 407 | 145 | 552 | 100.0 |

*Table 5(1)* presents a classification of all the occupations of the 848 members of Samples B and C, coded on the basis of the Registrar General's Socio-Economic Groups (1970). An additional distinction has been drawn between machine operation in the skilled and semi-skilled grades and work not involving this for reasons which will be apparent.

The largest category in both samples is that of semi-skilled, manual, non-machine work. It is considerably larger than the unskilled category, taking old and new workers together. However, many BII 'trial balloons,' the new workers engaged by the compassionate B employers, go into unskilled work. Machine workers are many fewer than non-machine workers, but none the less figure appreciably in the established workforce CI. Clerical grades are quite numerous in both samples; personal services and catering workers in the B Sample. The wide distribution of established employees in Sample CI testifies to the extent to which these workers remain in their previous occupations after a psychiatric episode.

The Schedule II samples of new employees illustrate employers' recruitment practice. In both BII and CII, recruitment into managerial, professional, supervisory, and technical occupations is infinitesimal. In Sample B, few ex-patients enter the skilled grade; considerable numbers are found in the clerical and catering and personal service grades; but the bulk of recruitment is into non-machine, semi-skilled work and labouring. In Sample C 148 employers recruit between them only seventeen ex-patients into the skilled grades. Thirty-four clerical workers, forty-two semi-skilled non-machine operators, and thirty unskilled workers make up the flimsy total. Sample D is coded on the Department of Employment's revised scheme, CODOT, the Classification of Occupations and Directory of Occupational Titles. Although it is stated to have 'considerable compatibility' with the 1970 classification, CODOT is in fact constructed on a quite different principle which provides no mechanism for latching-in the two systems. Sample D is therefore not comparable with Samples B and C; specifically, there is no possibility of comparing levels of manual skill in similar terms. It may be seen from *Table 5(2)*, however, that just over half the D employees fall into the four bottom classes of the table, which describe industrial shop floor jobs. This means that 43 per cent are engaged in a mixture of other work, which while not all non-manual, is not shop floor either. The point is worth making, because as has already been observed, there is a tendency for hospital personnel to equate the concept of work with work performed on the shop-floor and even with work on a conveyor belt.

Another indication of the type and absence of complexity of jobs being performed by Sample D employees is furnished by data on training. It was found that 60 per cent of these workers were trained on

Table 5(2)    *Occupations of members of Sample D*

| CODOT major occupational groups | no. | % |
|---|---|---|
| professional and related | 20 | 11.2 |
| clerical and related | 36 | 20.0 |
| selling | 5 | 2.8 |
| catering, cleaning, and personal services | 15 | 8.3 |
| farming, gardening, groundsmen | 2 | 1.1 |
| materials processing, making and repairing occupations excluding metals and electrical | 12 | 6.7 |
| processing, making, and repairing occupations, metal and electrical | 33 | 18.3 |
| assembly, inspection, packaging, painting etc. | 26 | 14.4 |
| transport operating, materials moving and storing, etc. | 22 | 12.2 |
| miscellaneous | 9 | 5.0 |
| | 180 | 100.0 |

the job; 13 per cent not at all. Only a quarter were in jobs for which a special course of training had been required.

## The question of machine work

One of the first theoretical prohibitions concerned machine work, which some twenty years ago was judged to be beyond long-term ex-patients' capacity. The Epsom Industrial Therapy Organisation, under the chairmanship of the managing director of a local precision engineering company, and with the assistance of his seconded crafts-men, set out specifically to scotch this idea (Epsom ITO *Annual Reports* 1966–75). Again, on visits to industrial units, sheltered workshops and factories, the researcher was shown an epileptic lad operating an enormous guillotine, and a schizophrenic man operating an enormous press, by medical officers keen to disprove machine work as being universally contra-indicated.

Turning to the survey data, attention must first be drawn to a notable paradox. It is that Remploy new employees, people so severely incapacitated as to be deemed incapable of work in open conditions, are much more likely to be operating machines than ex-patients working in ordinary conditions, not considered bad enough to be sheltered workers.

This finding is achieved by isolating the figures for categories 5–8 of the occupation groups comprising skilled and semi-skilled workers.

Table 5(3)    *Machine work undertaken*

|  | Sample A Remploy no. | % | Sample B hospital-notified employers no. | % | Sample C no. | % |
|---|---|---|---|---|---|---|---|
| 5 skilled machine operators | 20 | 16 | 5 | 5 | 5 | 8 |
| 6 skilled non-machine operators | 44 | 36 | 5 | 6 | 12 | 18 |
| 7 semi-skilled machine operators | 24 | 20 | 12 | 11 | 7 | 10 |
| 8 semi-skilled non-machine operators | 33 | 27 | 82 | 79 | 42 | 64 |
| total skilled and semi-skilled manual grades | 121 | 100 | 104 | 100 | 66 | 100 |

It may be seen that 36 per cent of Remploy's skilled (5) and semi-skilled (7) industrial former in-patient workers operate machines, in comparison with 16 per cent of the same grades in Sample B and 18 per cent in Sample C. The comparison may be pursued in even greater detail. For instance, seventeen of Remploy's forty-four machine operators are sewing machinists, and it could be said that sewing machinists are not what are commonly thought of as industrial machinists. But even subtracting the seventeen sewing machinists from the total, the remaining twenty-seven still amount to 22 per cent of these grades in comparison with Sample B's 16 per cent and Sample C's 18 per cent. Granted that Remploy is engaged exclusively in industrial manufacture, which Samples B and C are not, with the result that there may be more opportunities for non-machine work in these latter, the fact remains that the Remploy workers are actually operating these machines, the point which is being made here – though they may indeed be operating them at a slower pace than in open industry.

Does this then mean that ex-patients can after all operate machines with impunity? If so, which type of ex-patient? How are the machine operators diagnosed? Is it the case that psychotics only are debarred? In order to consider this possibility, the occupations of 389 established employees in Sample CI were analysed in relation to their diagnoses. The answer is surprising. Though the numbers involved at each occupational level are small, people diagnosed as psychotic are just as likely to be operating machines (9 or 12 per cent out of seventy-three) as are people diagnosed depressed (24 or 11 per cent out of 224) or as people diagnosed as neurotic (4 or 8 per cent out of fifty-three). Where the major difference lies is in the higher proportion of psychotics in the semi-skilled, non-machine grade and unskilled grade, and their corresponding lower proportion in the managerial and supervisory occupations compared with depressed and neurotic people.

So it is not simply a question of diagnosis, but it does indeed look as if machine operation is undertaken only by a minority of ex-patients. And, as we shall see, after relapses involving hospital admission, it is chiefly the skilled workers who have been found to lose their jobs as a result.

When the study of Sample D members was undertaken later, the opportunity was seized to investigate job skills and the tools and machines used. It turned out that a third of the thirty psychotics were setters (4) or operators (6): 35 per cent of the main depressive category (comprising those diagnosed as endogenous depression or depression not otherwise defined): 17 per cent of the reactive depressives: however, 22 per cent of the neurotics used non-powered hand tools or implements. A word of explanation is needed on the classification used to arrive at these results, since many jobs require a combination of skills. For example, a setter-operator sets his machine, operates it, and may well use pencil and paper in the course of dealing with a blue-print. To arrive at a simple categorization, the lesser skill has been subsumed in the greater. Thus the category of setter includes all setters whether combined with maintenance or operation, i.e. for the purposes of the above it was regarded as the top skill. The hand tool category comprized only those who use nothing but hand tools, thus excluding setters, operators, and minders who may also use hand tools.

Further defining capacities and skills, information was sought on the number of machines operated and the nature of the tools used. For this a senior member of the University engineering department was consulted to ensure the accurate coding of the more esoteric examples like 'dog-on-tube drawing benches.' Seventy-three of the 180 subjects used no

Table 5(4) CI: Distribution of occupation by diagnosis

| diagnosis | managerial and professional | | intermediate, supervisory, and technical | | clerical | | personal services and catering | | skilled manual machine operators | | skilled non-machine workers | | semi-skilled manual machine operators | | semi-skilled non-machine workers | | unskilled | | Total | |
|---|---|---|---|---|---|---|---|---|---|---|---|---|---|---|---|---|---|---|---|---|
| | no. | % | no. | % | no. | % | no. | % | no. | % | no. | % | no. | % | no. | % | no. | % | no. | % |
| psychoses | 3 | 4 | 3 | 4 | 9 | 12 | — | — | 3 | 4 | 5 | 7 | 6 | 8 | 30 | 41 | 14 | 19 | 73 | 19 |
| all types of depression | 29 | 13 | 20 | 9 | 39 | 17 | 3 | 1 | 9 | 4 | 23 | 10 | 15 | 7 | 55 | 25 | 31 | 14 | 224 | 57 |
| neurosis | 3 | 8 | 11 | 21 | 8 | 15 | — | — | 3 | 6 | 4 | 7 | 1 | 2 | 13 | 24 | 10 | 19 | 53 | 14 |
| alcoholism and addiction | 5 | 23 | 3 | 14 | 4 | 18 | 1 | 5 | 1 | 5 | 1 | 5 | 2 | 9 | 3 | 14 | 2 | 9 | 22 | 6 |
| other: including personality disorder, organic disorder, epilepsy, subnormality | 2 | 12 | 2 | 12 | 1 | 6 | — | — | 3 | 18 | — | — | 1 | 6 | 3 | 18 | 5 | 29 | 17 | 4 |
| total | 42 | 11 | 39 | 10 | 61 | 16 | 4 | 1 | 19 | 5 | 33 | 8 | 25 | 6 | 104 | 27 | 62 | 16 | 389 | 100 |

Table 5(5)  *Tools, machinery and equipment used by diagnosed ex-patients*

| diagnosis of ex-patients | non-powered | | | | powered | | | | total using tools | no tools mentioned | total |
|---|---|---|---|---|---|---|---|---|---|---|---|
| | hand | measuring tools and instruments | mech- anical | office | hand | machine tools | mechanical plant and tools | mass production machinery | | | |
| psychosis | 6 | 2 | 1 | 6 | 0 | 1 | 1 | 4 | 21 | 9 | 30 |
| depression | 9 | 3 | 1 | 6 | 2 | 6 | 10 | 4 | 41 | 27 | 68 |
| neurosis | 5 | 4 | 1 | 1 | 0 | 2 | 4 | 2 | 19 | 13 | 32 |
| reactive depression | 2 | 3 | 0 | 4 | 1 | 1 | 3 | 1 | 15 | 15 | 30 |
| other | 4 | 1 | 1 | 0 | 1 | 2 | 1 | 1 | 11 | 9 | 20 |
| total | 26 | 13 | 4 | 17 | 4 | 12 | 19 | 12 | 107 | 73 | 180 |

machines or tools at all. For the remainder, 107 specified one tool, thirty-two a second, and seven a third, most of the second tools being of the same type as the first. Some two-thirds of these were powered, one-third not. Considering the information in relation to employees' diagnoses it may be seen that only one-third of the psychotics in this sample used powered apparatus; between a third and a half of the neurotics; and over half of all depressives.

To summarize: machinery is operated by a minority of all ex-patients of all diagnoses in the 1974 study, and powered apparatus, which is what the discussion is about, by a minority also of the D study as a whole, but by over half of those diagnosed depressive. Thus there is no question of a general prohibition on the use of machinery, but an impression that it is beyond the capacity of many. How these approximate ratios compare with the working population at large it is of course impossible to say without matched controls.

## Slowness and paced work

Slowness has long been identified as a handicap of mental illness, whether caused by insufficiently fast mental processing of work data, ineffective co-ordination of hand and eye, or other deficient psycho-motor mechanism, or simply through lethargy induced by medication (Wadsworth *et al.* 1961). Such slowness, however caused, rules out participation in the lucrative bonuses to be earned on fast assembly tracks.

There is thus little doubt that getting their work up to an acceptable industrial tempo is a problem that ex-patients face; an idea of the extent of their difficulty may be gleaned from data relating to the representative C Sample. This is analysed below, and in view of the widely held belief that it is a difficulty faced particularly by schizophrenics, it is of interest to observe that depressives appear as the recipients of just as many complaints on this score. Only those diagnosed neurotic attract very few slow-work complaints.

If ex-patients find difficulty in working fast enough, then they will probably be unable to undertake what is known as paced work, that is piecework, or work performed on continuous production lines or moving belts. These will simply go too fast for them. The extent to which ex-patients are in fact engaged upon paced work was elicited in 1974. The fact that they were engaged on paced work does not necessarily mean they were successful at it, and some information on this aspect of the matter may also be deduced from the data. The paced workers and the non-paced workers lasted very nearly equally well in

Table 5(6)  Complaints about behaviour, slow work, and sickness absence by diagnosis

| diagnosis | number | | general complaints | | complaints about slow work | | other complaints* | | | sickness absence (%) |
|---|---|---|---|---|---|---|---|---|---|---|
| | 'old' employees | 'new' employees | 'old' employees complained of (%) | 'new' employees complained of (%) | 'old' employees complained of (%) | 'new' employees complained of (%) | odd behaviour (%) | disagreeable behaviour (%) | dangerous behaviour (%) | |
| psychoses | 71 | 28 | 66.2 | 50.0 | 29.6 | 14.3 | 40.4 | 10.1 | 9.1 | 18.1 |
| depression | 229 | 59 | 60.7 | 32.0 | 31.4 | 11.9 | 21.5 | 7.6 | 2.4 | 20.8 |
| neuroses | 53 | 24 | 50.9 | 12.5 | 11.3 | 4.2 | 10.4 | 5.2 | 1.3 | 26.0 |
| personality disorders | 7 | 9 | 85.7 | 66.7 | 28.6 | 22.2 | 56.2 | 25.0 | 0 | 12.5 |
| alcoholics/addicts | 23 | 12 | 60.9 | 58.3 | 30.4 | 0 | 25.7 | 17.1 | 2.9 | 34.3 |
| others | 10 | 6 | 80.0 | 50.0 | 30.0 | 75.0 | 29.4 | 29.4 | 11.8 | 11.8 |
| all diagnoses | 393 | 139 | 61.3 | 38.1 | 28.2 | 12.2 | 25.0 | 9.6 | 3.8 | 21.4 |

* Complaints about both old and new employees.
Source: Wansbrough and Cooper 1977

Table 5(7)  *Percentage of ex-patient workers engaged in paced work*

| sample | % of paced workers | total workers |
|---|---|---|
| Remploy I | 20 | 45 |
| Remploy II | 18 | 142 |
| Sample B I | 4 | 54 |
| Sample B II | 9 | 242 |
| Sample C I | 22 | 407 |
| Sample C II | 21 | 145 |

employment (Remploy II 83 per cent paced, and 85 per cent non-paced, BII 59 per cent paced and 62 per cent non-paced being respectively still in employment at the time of the enquiry). In Remploy the paced workers were complained about significantly less than the non-paced workers, probably because the most recovered ex-patients were able to undertake paced work and were complained about less because they were less ill. On the other hand, in the open conditions of Sample CII, the paced workers were complained about significantly more (5 per cent level) for slow work. Not many workers were taken off paced work as the result of a hospitalization episode: in CI, ninety-one were engaged in paced work before hospitalization and eighty-six after it. The fact that only 9 per cent of BII's work-force were on paced work is further evidence, surely, that these patients were less well recovered than those in the other samples.

For Sample D paced work as such was not a subject of investigation but methods of payment were. Of the 180 subjects in this sample, 4 per cent were on piece-work, 21 per cent on incentive bonus, but the majority of 71 per cent were paid a flat wage. (5 per cent were paid by a mixture of methods). These proportions tally quite well with the data above (see *Table 5(7)*), for paced work is of course remunerated by incentive methods. It is interesting that as high a proportion of psychotics as of subjects diagnosed depressive or neurotic are paid by incentive bonus.

Correspondence from employers and evidence from our subsidiary studies confirm the survey figures just considered. From all these quarters came reports that, for many ex-patients, paced work is unsuccessful. Borough surveyors did not know what to do now that time-study has come to road-sweeping. The manager of an East Anglian canning factory found that his team of women on bonus would not accept a lame duck. That the fast moving tracks in engineering and elsewhere are frequently contra-indicated was also found in our own case studies. In fact the evidence of all our data confirms this accepted handicap, contributing an element of quantification.

## Manual versus non-manual work

Another distinction grew up, the distinction between manual work and non-manual work. Anyone surveying the rehabilitation scene could observe that the work performed in hospital industrial therapy units was predominantly, if not exclusively, manual rather than clerical. The same could be said of ERCs, though of recent years a determined attempt has been made to redress the balance by introducing more clerical and accountancy training. So far as hospital industrial units go, these were not intended to be vocational (it was said), and the repetitive sub-contract work provided was intended to do no more than reintroduce a patient to systematic working habits. This may well have been so, but it is the case that sub-contract work pays, particularly engineering sub-contract work, and thus furnishes the essential financial motivation. This fact, rather than any theoretical orientation towards manual work, is in our view much more likely to account for its predominance. In any event, it never occurred to us to consider work suitability in the uncompromising terms of the antithesis above until one day we received a letter. The Senior Medical Officer in charge of the occupational health service of a large city corporation wrote on the basis of his experience of 16,000 employees scattered over more than twenty-five departments. 'Clerical or administrative posts' he observed, 'where team work and inter-personal relationships are essential, are not successful, and at best are tolerated only. Manual occupations, particularly if a man is working on his own, at his own home with sympathetic supervision are most likely to succeed provided that sickness absences are not excessive.' We looked around.

Two jobs in Sample B clearly identified as clerical both appeared as failures. One ex-patient created havoc in an architect's office: the other, though at the time of our enquiry still just tolerated as a telephonist, had been found to be at the bottom of all the petty squabbles in the building where she worked. Both these cases might be attributed to the personality difficulties which can obtrude so much more dramatically within the confines of an office than on the wide open spaces of the factory floor.

The statistical data were therefore examined with a view to confirming or disproving these observations. Was there any evidence that non-manual workers were complained about more, either for odd or disagreeable behaviour, or because they worked more slowly or were more frequently absent sick, than manual workers?

No fewer than twenty-four tables have been assembled referring to these hypotheses and twenty-two of them showed the differences between the two groups to be insignificant using the indices at our disposal. In fact the remarkable thing was the similarity of experience. The two exceptions relate to the Sample C Schedule II groups of 145 new employees – the most 'open' sample in the 1974 research. Here the manual workers were complained about significantly more often than the non-manual workers and they were also the subject of more complaints specifically on account of sickness absence. Certainly, this evidence does not support that of the Corporation medical officer. But it is also worth looking at the manual/non-manual distinction from another standpoint – the analysis by 'type of organization', that is to say, whether an employee is working in industry, or in a professional, scientific or commercial milieu, in distribution or a service, or the field of public administration and defence.

Table 5(8)    *Analysis of complaints by type of organization*

|  | industry no. | % | pro-fessional scientific commercial no. | % | distri-bution no. | % | public adminis-tration defence no. | % | other no. | % |
|---|---|---|---|---|---|---|---|---|---|---|
| no complaints | 121 | 37 | 5 | 18 | 15 | 44 | 12 | 60 | 0 | 0 |
| some complaints | 195 | 60 | 23 | 82 | 19 | 56 | 7 | 35 | 1 | 100 |
| not known | 8 | 3 | 0 | 0 | 0 | 0 | 1 | 5 | 0 | 0 |
|  | 324 | 100 | 28 | 100 | 34 | 100 | 20 | 100 | 1 | 100 |

Though the numbers are not large, they do seem to show that people working in the public administration and defence sector are complained about significantly less than those who work in industry (representing the average); and also that those working in the commercial world are complained about significantly more. Could this mean that office-type work is indeed contra-indicated? On the other hand, why should the public administration world – which is largely the nationalized world, complain significantly less about their ex-patients? Thus the evidence was contradictory, on the subject of the relative 'success' of those in manual and non-manual occupations, and it was decided that it ought to be further investigated in the next study.

This next study, culminating in the D results, consisted of a slice of life, a year's experience lived by 180 subjects. Of these 20 per cent were clerical workers and 11 per cent held managerial or professional posts.

Spells of psychiatric sickness absence, with or without renewed hospital admission, seemed for this study the best indicators of 'success'; the absence of such spells indicated at least satisfactory attendance at work, which as shown in Chapter 7, represents a major achievement. Was there anything to suggest in Sample D that clerical or non-manual staff had more or less sickness absence than manual staff? In fact there was, indirectly. The figures below show that people sharing an office with up to four others have more sickness absence than people working on their own, or with a larger number of people. However, when the size of working group is considered, the distinction irrespective of location disappears; people whose work is performed in a small group, not necessarily in an office, do not take significantly more time off than others. For this state of affairs an explanation could be that a shared office becomes intolerable because of the close proximity of the occupants, whereas a small group, say on a shop floor, can breathe a great deal more freely.

Table 5(9)  *Percentage of workers having psychiatric sickness absence, by work situation*

|  | *own office* | *shared office (up to 4 others)* | *defined area* | *roving com- mission* | *open air; driving* |
|---|---|---|---|---|---|
| workers having sickness absence | 18 | 42 | 25 | 23 | 17 |

Table 5(10)  *Percentage of workers having psychiatric sickness absence, by group size*

|  | *works alone* | *up to 4* | *5-14* | *15+* |
|---|---|---|---|---|
| workers having psychiatric sickness absence | 28 | 29 | 24 | 20 |

All in all, the position seems to be that non-manual work, which is usually clerical work, is by its nature work suitable for many ex-patients, and we have examples of people who have found jobs of this sort away from the pressure of the production process. But there is a strong indication that relations can become strained in the confines of a small office.

## Situations and responsibilities

Professional colleagues on the committee which helped to plan the record-keeping study suggested other aspects of the working environment might present difficulty. They visualized potentially dangerous situations, potentially expensive situations, potential clashes resulting from strict disciplinary codes, responsibilities for this and that which might be found onerous and oppressive. The extent to which D ex-patients' work in practice involved them in these matters is set out in *Table 5(11)*. The proportions involved are not large but are substantial

Table 5(11)   *180 D study ex-patients' involvement in certain responsibilities and situations*

|  | *no.* | *%* |
|---|---|---|
| taking responsibility for the work of others | 27 | 15 |
| handling money, i.e. cash | 15 | 8 |
| responsibility for expenditure (but not handling cash) | 9 | 5 |
| use of machinery which if damaged through negligence might be expensive to repair (costs or time) | 41 | 23 |
| contact with or access to dangerous drugs | 7 | 4 |
| contact with noxious substances, e.g. acids or molten metal | 14 | 8 |
| contact with substances or equipment which might cause explosion, fire, or flood | 17 | 9 |
| working height above 6ft 6ins (e.g. painters or scaffolders) | 10 | 6 |
| none of these | 68 | 38 |

*Note*: Some ex-patients are involved in more than one of the above. Percentages therefore exceed 100.

enough to confirm that these situations exist. It may also be confirmed that ex-patients survive in jobs with specific disciplinary rules, the sanction for which is usually dismissal, whether these are embodied in complete company rule books or simply deal with smoking or the wearing of protective clothing. Over a third of the 180 employees manage to work with these rules. Finally, what could be the effect on a frail personality of a room without a view? Or of continuous loud noise? Or, even more disturbing according to some, intermittent, unpredictable noise? Is the impact of these detectable by statistical means? Our data in fact suggest no connection between physical conditions and the onset of relapses, nor of extensive sickness absences. They simply demonstrate that ex-patients are currently holding down jobs in these less than ideal physical surroundings.

Table 5(12)   *Percentage of 180 D study ex-patients working in certain physical conditions*

| view | % |
|---|---|
| windows with open view | 36 |
| skylight or restricted outlook such as frosted glass | 27 |
| artificial light only | 20 |
| not applicable | 17 |

| noise | % |
|---|---|
| comfortably noisy or very quiet | 64 |
| continuously very noisy (speech impossible or have to shout) | 9 |
| intermittently very noisy | 20 |
| not applicable | 7 |

## Task and role performance

The current fashion is to draw a distinction between task and role performance. The psychiatrically ill person, it is said, finds particular difficulty in fulfilling his worker role, whereas he has been shown to be not inferior to other ERC rehabilitees in accurately completing prescribed tasks; therefore task performance presents less difficulty than role fulfilment (Wing *et al.* 1964). Is this a useful way of considering the real life experience of ex-patients at work? What insights does it yield?

It must first be said that no analysis in terms of role and task was undertaken in our studies. What we have are indications of certain factors often regarded as role or task elements. Thus there is the overall worker role as distinct from the patient role, or, for some women, the housewife role. Certainly our data may be interpreted as confirming the difficulty that ex-patients have of adapting to the generalized worker role and of regarding this as appropriate to themselves; this seems a useful concept. For instance it is exemplified in the difficulty that ex-patients experience in turning up for work at all, particularly in the first few weeks. This is not surprising. Going to a new job can be an ordeal for even the most robust personality, and many and fanciful are the induction courses dreamed up by personnel departments to ease the process. So, many more workers (Schedule II) simply fail to turn up. Even in Remploy where new employees are almost without exception introduced by the DRO and where a three-month trial period is worked, difficulty is experienced. 'It is essential that some interested person should co-operate with management in order to ensure attendance at work, getting them up etc. especially during the first few weeks,' wrote a Remploy works manager. Open employers time and again emphasized the same problem in the correspondence which forms such a useful background to our quantified findings. As to these, an analysis of the reasons for terminating employment of all the newly engaged (Schedule II) Remploy, B and C employees showed that 17 per cent of all who left just simply failed to report at all. In the D study, new workers would get off the works bus and wander round town rather than face work, a form of behaviour also demonstrated by members of the long-term unemployed sample in the Southampton Enclave Experiment (1978) who had clearly, as a result of their long detachment from the worker role, ceased to regard themselves in this light.

The fact that it is the new workers, rather than the established ones, who encounter this difficulty, is clear from our figures; for only one out of the sixty-two old employees in B and C whose employment terminated, was listed as having failed to report. The figure also confirms a widely appreciated fact, that ex-patients do best if after hospitalization they are able to return to their old jobs.

## Source of referral and introduction to work

For those who are obliged to seek a new job (Schedule II workers) the importance of the actual process of introducing an ex-patient to his new situation has also long been recognized. We considered it up hill and down dale in 1974 and as part of this consideration analysed 'success' (defined as still continuing employment) by methods of introduction and by sources of referral. We asked: who is it that effects this introduction? Whence comes the ex-patient thus introduced? And do these factors point to any conclusions as to the source of referral of the most 'successful' employees? For the Remploy and B samples who obtain virtually all their recruits from an identical source, viz. the DRO for Remploy, and the hospitals for Sample B, this could not be a fruitful line of enquiry since no comparison was possible. But for the exposed CII sample of 145 new employees in open industry, an important result became quickly apparent.

First the matter was investigated using the complaints index, from which it was shown quite clearly that the ex-patients who had been sent from the employment exchange after a period of unemployment were complained about less than those who came direct from the hospitals, and indeed also less than those who came from another job or training.

The really interesting results were however to be observed when the Method of Introduction and Source of Referral factors were set against the Employment index. On this index, the ex-patients referred from the hospitals lasted less well than the ex-patients entering employment via agencies other than the hospitals and both these results were so strongly marked as to be significant statistically at the 5 per cent level. Whereas the proportion of all 145 ex-patients still in employment is 82 per cent (and those who came via the employment exchanges or in answer to advertisements lasted proportionally better than this) the record of the hospital entrants was less enviable, since only 38 per cent of them were still employed. A similar trend was to be remarked when the source of referral was investigated. In this case, the percentage of hospital-referred ex-patients still employed was only 57 per cent whereas for ex-patients from all other sources the percentages were 83 per cent or over. This result also is significant ($P = 0.01$). 91 per cent of those who came from another job or training were still employed and 83 per cent of those who had had a spell of unemployment.

Taken into consideration together this batch of tables indicates that ex-patients direct from hospital entering open competitive employment show up at a disadvantage compared with those who have been out of hospital some time – even if these latter have been unemployed. The conclusion seems inescapable that hospital preparation alone is insufficient and the sudden transition from patient into worker role too great; and that the slow process of rehabilitation for those who have been mentally ill cannot satisfactorily be hurried.

## Social relations

Another major element in 'role' success has been identified as competence in social relations. Evidently some of the same factors apply here as have been considered in relation to the manual work discussion. People working in shared offices seem to take more time off sick than people working alone or in more spacious surroundings.

Our data illustrate the extent to which jobs involving interpersonal relationships are in fact being undertaken. Thus it is of interest to note where Sample D employees work. Just one half do so in their defined area in office, shop or workshop where it may be surmised that they can

Table 5(13)  Sample C II: still continuing employment judged by method of introduction

| | friend etc. | | advert etc. | | employment exchange | | DRO | | hospital | | other | | total | |
|---|---|---|---|---|---|---|---|---|---|---|---|---|---|---|
| | no. | % | no. | % | no. | % | no. | % | no. | % | no. | % | no. | % |
| still employed | 11 | 69 | 43 | 91 | 41 | 89 | 2 | 100 | 5 | 38 | 14 | 93 | 116 | 83 |
| total workers | 16 | 100 | 47 | 100 | 46 | 100 | 2 | 100 | 13 | 100 | 15 | 100 | 139 | 100 |

Table 5(14)  Sample C II: still continuing employment judged by source of referral

| | direct from hospital | | local authority day centre | | other job or training | | after un-employment | | other | | not known | | total |
|---|---|---|---|---|---|---|---|---|---|---|---|---|---|
| | no. | % | no. | % | no. | % | no. | % | no. | % | no. | % | |
| still employed | 16 | 57 | 1 | 100 | 49 | 91 | 39 | 83 | 5 | 83 | 1 | 100 | 111 |
| total workers | 28 | 100 | 1 | 100 | 54 | 100 | 47 | 100 | 6 | 100 | 1 | 100 | 137 |

to a great extent exercise their own discretion as to the amount of social interchange they wish to engage in. 37 per cent hold a roving commission, or work in the open air, or drive, or work in a mixture of these situations, which again would seem to offer scope for solitariness if this is preferred. 6 per cent have their own offices, leaving only 11 per cent who share with up to four others, and, as we have seen, look as if they cannot withstand the pressure. The size of their working group was also investigated and it was found that two-thirds work in large groups with five or more mates or colleagues: 8 per cent work alone, and a quarter with a group of up to four others. It has already been remarked that subjects working in these small groups do not appear to take a disproportionate amount of sick leave, the implication being that a small group on the shop floor is tolerable, whereas a small group in the closer proximity of an office is not.

The extent of communication with others necessitated for the performance of a job was an area on which data was also assembled, particularly having in mind comments from employers about the inadvisibility of ex-patients working in contact with the public. *Table 5(15)* shows these communication patterns. It is certainly the case that

Table 5(15)  *Communication patterns: percentage of subjects in communication*

| with | face to face % | telephone % | written % |
|---|---|---|---|
| superiors | 80 | 49. | 45 |
| colleagues | 80 | 46 | 35 |
| subordinates | 20 | 16 | 10 |
| public | 14 | 17 | 14 |
| none of these | 0.5 | 45 | 50 |

ex-patients are in jobs where they communicate less often with the public and with subordinates than they do with their superiors or their colleagues. Of course, by no means everyone has got a subordinate: nor does the public penetrate most factories. Nor, unfortunately, do we have controls to show the normal pattern. But the picture presented is not without interest. Also of interest is the breakdown by diagnosis of the factor 'Face to face communication with the public.' *Table 5(16)* shows that a very slightly lower percentage of psychotics are in jobs necessitating face to face contact with the public than the percentages of depressives, but the difference is not all that great. Evidently a

Table 5(16)    *Face to face communication with public by diagnostic group*

|  | psychoses % | depressions % | neuroses % | other % | all % |
|---|---|---|---|---|---|
| public | 13 | 15 | 18 | 6 | 15 |
| no public | 83 | 79 | 75 | 94 | 80 |
| not applicable | 4 | 6 | 7 | 0 | 5 |

proportion of people diagnosed as schizophrenic do function adequately in this regard.

Analysis of these jobs also serves to direct attention to the usefulness or otherwise, of attempting to distinguish role from task once we break into the wide world of open employment. In the laboratory conditions of an ERC or hospital workshop, where the work is predominantly bench type manual or clerical, the antithesis is clearly valid and useful. In the wide world, as we have seen, the role element appears to form an integral part of so many of the tasks which make up a day's work, that the distinction may be found artificial and puzzling. For the open employer and his welfare officer, might it not be simpler to accept that Wilf has great difficulty getting up in the morning, is likely to be of a solitary rather than gregarious disposition; and, most important, that these traits rather than outbursts of violence are the characteristic residual symptoms of a one-time severe illness?

## Support at work: conditions, devices, and professional support

These discussions of the supposed limitations on the kind of work ex-patients can do indicate that there is no smoke without fire, that certain areas do indeed present more difficulty than others, and that the pressure of attempting to work at all turns out, when the crunch comes, to be more than 17 per cent of new employees can face. This is not new, and the next question to ask is: to what extent can ex-patients be helped to survive by features of the working organization and environment? What kind of support can they look for, and how effective is it?

### The trial period

One way of cushioning the impact of a new job is to lessen the finality of a commitment to it. A trial period is in any case a useful safeguard for employer and employed now that formal contracts of employment are required and the Employment Protection Act now provides a six month trial period. Also, the Employment Services Division have introduced a twelve month experimental Job Introduction Scheme effectively embodying a trial period.

So far as our own samples go, for Remploy factories a three month trial period is mandatory for everybody. As regards Samples B and C, whether or not an ex-patient had worked a trial period had no identifiable effect on his 'success' when looked at statistically. However, a medical officer in an old-established confectionery firm with a caring tradition said he found that the trial period enabled them to exclude without rancour those who proved themselves incapable. Some of these even wrote to thank the firm for the chance. In short, commonsense and some correspondence applaud the device of the trial period but, as measured by the indices at our disposal, it cannot be shown statistically to have increased an employee's chances of success.

*Hours and conditions*

How many hours are worked, and when they are worked, constitute an important element of the conditions surrounding a job, and they represent an area in which medical representations may appropriately be made, which is not the case with regard to pay matters. The hours and shifts worked by members of the six 1974 samples were therefore investigated. It was found that only a handful were working part-time, (3 per cent of old employees and 8 per cent of new ones). The great majority, including all Remploy employees, worked full-time and of these nearly half worked over-time if required. Many more worked shifts, where these were in operation, than were excused them, although no shifts at all were worked in about four-fifths of all the jobs, so that it is possible that ex-patients were purposely placed in these jobs in the first place.

It seemed likely that variations might occur in working conditions according to the diagnosis of the worker; and that if employers with access to medical advice were to know the diagnosis of an employee, they would be that much better able to help him. The C Samples were then analysed by diagnosis and descriptive data on the hours worked by the 534 members of these open employment samples were collected. The highest incidence of part-time employment was found in the depressive group. Overtime, as necessary, was worked by 43 per cent of old employees and 36 per cent of new ones. No diagnostic group appeared to be ducking overtime.

Data on shift working was available for 527 members of these same two C Samples and showed shift work to be evidently a more

Table 5(17)  *Percentage distribution of working hours by diagnosis*

| diagnosis | 'old' employees | | | | 'new' employees | | | |
|---|---|---|---|---|---|---|---|---|
| | number | part-time | full-time | over-time* | number | part-time | full-time | overtime* |
| psychoses | 74 | 2.7 | 51.4 | 45.9 | 28 | 7.1 | 71.4 | 21.4 |
| depression | 228 | 4.4 | 52.2 | 43.4 | 58 | 12.1 | 51.7 | 36.2 |
| neuroses | 54 | 1.8 | 42.6 | 55.6 | 24 | 4.2 | 62.5 | 33.3 |
| personality disorders | 7 | 0 | 57.1 | 42.9 | 9 | 33.3 | 55.6 | 11.1 |
| alcoholics/addicts | 23 | 0 | 60.9 | 39.1 | 12 | 0 | 25.0 | 75.0 |
| others | 10 | 0 | 70.0 | 30.0 | 7 | 0 | 57.1 | 42.9 |
| all diagnoses | 396 | 3.3 | 53.5 | 43.2 | 138 | 8.0 | 55.8 | 36.2 |

* Overtime worked if required.

demanding requirement. Quite a high proportion were excused it altogether – 26 per cent of new employees and 44 per cent of old ones, a difference which in itself is of interest as illustrating the lenient attitude adopted by employers towards their existing workers. As to specific diagnoses, alcoholics, addicts, and people diagnosed as neurotic undertook shifts relatively more often than did psychotics and depressives. This incidentally confirmed the comment of a participating medical officer who had found shift work on a production line to be a difficult milieu for schizophrenics or severe anxiety cases.

### Consultation with trade unions

It was suggested also that an employee's chances might be improved by a factor of trade union consultation at local level. (At national level eminently liberal and reasonable views have been voiced.) In three out of the four B and C open employment samples, it made no difference to an ex-patient's 'success' whether or not such trade union consultation had taken place, but in Sample B II, where twelve ex-patients were employed where consultation had taken place, and 102 in firms where no consultation had taken place, it appeared that trade union consultation had led to more complaints rather than fewer (5 per cent level of significance). But the figures are rather small for too much importance to be attached to this curious, potentially disturbing finding.

Perhaps more significant is the experience of operating the Southampton Enclave, when local trade union officers, their enthusiasm aroused by a visit to the local psychiatric hospital, and their confidence sustained by dealing with a voluntary body which they trusted, provided quite invaluable support at shop floor level and in stimulating employers (Southampton Enclave Team 1978). The important Lincolnshire rehabilitation scheme of the 1960s offers another case in point (Wansbrough 1973). Over a hundred former patients were offered employment in a large local plant, which could never have been achieved, in the view of the medical officer of the factory, had he not first fully explained the scheme and sought trade union co-operation at a local delegate meeting. This indeed seems a field where trade unions could properly forward the interests of their more vulnerable members more extensively than has hitherto been the case.

### The support of professionals

The support needed by someone who has undergone acute mental illness is not often minutely defined. It can range from a cup of tea and a cigarette to more professional therapeutic counselling, adjustment of drug dosage, investigation of home circumstances, and the mobilization of state and local authority benefits and services right through to arrangements for readmission to hospital. In the open ended comment which forms an important part of our evidence, many of our respondents testified to the time consuming support which they have felt obliged to proffer to ex-psychiatric patients. One Remploy manager thought that Remploy foremen should be paid extra for supervising them. In the larger units support is hived off to professionals: doctors, nurses, personnel, and welfare officers. Besides these, in any sized unit may be found first aiders and 'uncles', defined as mature and sympathetic workmates appointed to keep an eye on a newcomer. It was decided to look at firms staffed with medical and welfare officers to see whether ex-patients fared better there than in those firms without them. All Remploy factories have part-time medical officers, but only four have State Registered Nurses, the majority employing State Enrolled Nurses or trained First Aiders (forty-eight out of sixty-four). Nineteen have personnel or welfare officers, probably not professional, as Remploys are too small, and twenty an 'uncle' system. Twelve factories appeared to have no nurse or first aider of any description, and the medical officers being local general practititoners are more often away from the factory than in it. These figures are detailed because considering the nature of the workforce, such provision may be thought frugal although the factories are small. One Remploy manager told the researcher he had never felt so isolated as in this job.

What was their effect? On the 142 new workers, nil: the presence of SRNs, SENs, First Aiders, Personnel or Welfare Officers made absolutely no difference, as measured on the employment and complaints indices, to the 142 new Remploy workers in the sample. On the forty-five old ex-patients, the effect was mixed. Where personnel officers, SENs or First Aiders were in post, a significantly smaller proportion of ex-patients were complained about than in those Remploys without them. Also there was a trend for the presence of these officers to be associated with ex-patients remaining in their jobs. But as for uncles, quite the reverse. An uncle system appeared to be associated with ex-patients leaving employment (5 per cent level of significance) and generating complaints.

Much the same uncle effect was to be observed in the open B and C samples: the more uncles there were, the more complaints were to be heard. Sample C was invariably staffed by doctors, nurses, and personnel officers but uncles were found in only a quarter of these firms. Although there were more complaints about ex-patients in firms with uncles than without them, it was found that a significantly higher percentage of ex-patients remained in their jobs (5 per cent level: 96 per cent v 86 per cent). The picture persists of a hard-pressed uncle exerting a steadying influence but probably complaining freely about his charge.

What can be made of this rather confusing evidence? One thing is clear. Ex-patients do not 'succeed' best under the aegis of the full panoply of supportive staff – whether these be professionally qualified or amateur, like uncles. And according to the figures, personnel and welfare officers seem to be of most help. Possible explanations spring to mind. One is that the firms without all these officers are the small firms where the personal touch is to be found everywhere and does not have to be consigned to professionals, and where an ex-patient may well find an unpressured, satisfactory niche. The second possibility is that professionals may use their expertise to disqualify ex-patients rather than to assist them. A third possibility is that by their very presence they generate or attract complaints, as representing somebody appropriate for people to complain to.

Yet having analysed the figures, it must be reported that, in the course of the research, contact was made with individual doctors and nurses who, quite clearly, provide much effective support to ex-patient employees. Whether this points to the inadequacy of statistical method, or whether these doctors and nurses provide the exception that proves the rule, or whether indeed their efforts should be seen statistically as serving to counteract the disadvantages of large-scale organization, cannot be decided on the evidence available.

### Maintenance medication

A major cause of breakdown in discharged patients is believed to be failure to persevere with self-medication, and the default rate in taking prescribed drugs has been shown to be as high as 48 per cent (Willcox *et al.* 1965). One of the services that professionally qualified medical or welfare staff might perform for an ex-patient, it was thought, would be to remind him to take his tablets and to go for his injections. In the event, we found that over half the Remploys 'remind', a third of B employers do so, and over half the C employers. But the results of their so doing are neither uniform nor expected, nor strongly marked. In general, the tendency is for ex-patients who have been reminded to take their drugs to attract more complaints than those not reminded, suggesting (as seems very likely) that they are less well recovered. Indeed, one industrial medical officer, commenting on his questionnaire, refuses to contemplate as fit for employment any ex-patient out of hospital under eighteen months and incapable of self-medication.

## Summary

None of the samples from which these data are drawn is random, so that generalization to the whole range of industrial experience is not permissible. But at least the suggested prohibitions of various types of work are seen to be not universally applicable, even for schizophrenics. Employees are to be found engaged in each supposedly contra-indicated activity, in each contra-indicated environment. Also, since the bias in the D sample is known to be towards severity of illness, the probability is that the picture painted is more pessimistic than the true state of affairs. Though it looks as if employers might, in view of Remploy experience, take a chance and give more ex-patients the chance of achieving the higher rewards associated with machine operation, the figures show that this is undertaken at present by only a minority of ex-patients, which includes those diagnosed schizophrenic. The probability is that the pace of machine-work in open conditions, as distinct from Remploy, is indeed too fast for most of them. This is suggested also by considering the matter in terms of paced work, but that the quite substantial minority found to be undertaking paced work also includes psychotics is a point of some importance.

So far we have been referring to manual work. The suitability of non-manual work for ex-patients has also been as extensively investigated as our data would allow. Clearly some clerical jobs offer a satisfactory niche to which for example, employees identified in Chapter 8 were transferred when the pace of manual work became too hot for them. On the other hand, clerical workers in small offices are apt to take more sick leave than those deployed elsewhere, and the hypothesis has to be entertained that working in these potentially trying conditions may not offer a good milieu. There is a certain amount of evidence to suggest that subjects simply get on each other's nerves. Other aspects of the environment suggested as presenting possible difficulty do not, judged by the indices we have, do so, but are experienced by admittedly only a minority of ex-patients.

The records in our possession, and in particular the year-long records of the 'Slice of Life' D study do not suggest discrimination on the part of employers in the sense that they are withholding promotion. Rather, the impression is that they are striving to keep on their ex-patients in whatever jobs they can do. Transfers are made, shifts avoided. Rule of thumb juggling is undertaken as a matter of course by medical and personnel staff, not only for mentally ill people but for physically disabled and elderly long-service operatives unable to withstand the heat. The economics of such practices, and the possible resultant over-manning have not so far as we know been systematically investigated, the unspoken thought being that the less said about it, the better.

# 6

## Behavioural characteristics
## and employers' reactions

Nearly two-thirds of our samples of known ex-patients exhibit no unusual behavioural characteristics for firms to react to. We suspect that more still, having successfully concealed their history of illness, also pursue their course, as do colleagues who have not been thus afflicted. But the eccentric conduct of a minority in our samples has evoked a variety of responses of which the only predictable one is the tolerant treatment accorded to long service employees. In general, it looks as if management's understandable concern to get the work out is less pressing than their fear of upsetting the workforce. Foremen, in their recognized double-bind situation, have to weigh production demands against the humane personnel policies to which in all probability they have also been instructed to adhere. Organized labour seems more apprehensive about what it regards as a potential cheap labour threat than about oddity of behaviour, though there are notable exceptions to this attitude. The individual worker is quite likely to take the line encountered in more than one visit: 'Why shouldn't the poor b——be allowed to earn a living same as us?'

There seemed room in the formal studies, therefore, to examine employers' reactions systematically. What sort of complaints did they make? Who made them? As already suggested, it matters a great deal to an employer how acceptable to each other his employees are or whether one of their number works so slowly that he holds up the others; indeed, whether he turns up for work at all. So crucial was this question of acceptability that we decided to treat complaints, or their absence, as an index of 'successful' resettlement in employment. After specific consultation on this point with Dr Peter Sainsbury, we agreed to ask the respondents in the 1973 survey if they knew of complaints about slow work, excessive sickness absence, or odd behaviour on the part of their ex-patients. An example of disagreeable behaviour would be compulsive eating or picking about in dustbins. To talk to oneself rated as odd behaviour. A physical attack or violent episode constituted dangerous behaviour. The results for the six samples are set out in *Table 6(1)*.

Most frequently mentioned were complaints of slow work or odd behaviour (top of the list at three times each). Sickness absence was also a frequent cause of complaint, usually third in the ranking order. For all six samples dangerous behaviour was most seldom the reason for complaint and for all the samples but one, disagreeable behaviour was the second most seldom. Thus the violent characteristics portrayed on stage and screen rarely occurred in real life. Rather the complaints were of inadequacy and oddity. It is also clear that employers in the open C sample, and also in Remploy, seem prepared to tolerate 'complained of' old employees to a greater degree than they are prepared to tolerate 'complained of' new employees. In Sample B this is not the case, but as will be made clear, Sample B II is revealed as an unrecovered group in most respects, so that this is not surprising.

The propensity of an ex-patient to attract complaints was found to correlate not only with 'old' or 'new' employment status (p = 0.05) but also in the C sample with diagnosis (*Table 6(2)*). The few employees with a personality disorder diagnosis were the subjects of most complaints; perhaps surprisingly those diagnosed as psychotic, alcoholic, or drug addicts attracted only slightly more complaints than employees diagnosed as depressive. People with a neurosis diagnosis were complained about least. Overall, 55 per cent of the C sample attracted complaints for one or more of the matters listed.

Complaints about slow work varied significantly with diagnosis. Again there were more complaints about 'old' employees than 'new' employees – 28 per cent compared to 12 per cent. Those diagnosed as depressive were complained about for slow work most, more often than those with a psychotic or personality disorder diagnosis. Only a small proportion of addicts and people diagnosed as neurotic were thought to work too slowly. The pattern is remarkably similar for both 'old' and 'new' employees.

On the subject of behaviour at work, the overall picture was that 75 per cent of these employees attracted no complaints on account of odd behaviour, 90 per cent attracted none for disagreeable behaviour and 96 per cent attracted no complaints for dangerous behaviour. The patterns of incidence of these behavioural traits are very similar for both 'old' and 'new' employees.

Where odd behaviour was complained of it was found to be

Table 6(1) Percentage of members of the six samples attracting complaints in five specific areas

| | Remploy | | Sample B (employers liaising with hospitals) | | Sample C (occupational health doctors) | |
|---|---|---|---|---|---|---|
| nature of complaint | (i) 45 old employees | (ii) 142 new employees | (i) 54 old employees | (ii) 242 new employees | (i) 407 old employees | (ii) 145 new employees |
| slow work | 31 | 39 | 15 | 25 | 28 | 12 |
| disagreeable behaviour | 27 | 8 | 15 | 9 | 10 | 7 |
| dangerous behaviour | 7 | 4 | 8 | 4 | 4 | 1 |
| odd behaviour | 55 | 30 | 28 | 24 | 27 | 18 |
| sickness absence | 29 | 20 | 13 | 11 | 23 | 16 |
| | — | — | — | — | — | — |
| total complained of | 82 | 62 | 46 | 52 | 61 | 38 |
| no complaints | 18 | 38 | 54 | 48 | 39 | 62 |

*percentage complained of*

Table 6(2)  *Complaints about behaviour, slow work, and sickness absence by diagnosis*

| diagnosis | number | | general complaints | | complaints about slow work | | other complaints* | | | sickness absence (%) |
|---|---|---|---|---|---|---|---|---|---|---|
| | 'old' employees | 'new' employees | 'old' employees complained of (%) | 'new' employees complained of (%) | 'old' employees complained of (%) | 'new' employees complained of (%) | odd behaviour (%) | disagreeable behaviour (%) | dangerous behaviour (%) | |
| psychoses | 71 | 28 | 66.2 | 50.0 | 29.6 | 14.3 | 40.4 | 10.1 | 9.1 | 18.1 |
| depression | 229 | 59 | 60.7 | 32.0 | 31.4 | 11.9 | 21.5 | 7.6 | 2.4 | 20.8 |
| neuroses | 53 | 24 | 50.9 | 12.5 | 11.3 | 4.2 | 10.4 | 5.2 | 1.3 | 26.0 |
| personality disorders | 7 | 9 | 85.7 | 66.7 | 28.6 | 22.2 | 56.2 | 25.0 | 0 | 12.5 |
| alcoholics/ addicts | 23 | 12 | 60.9 | 58.3 | 30.4 | 0 | 25.7 | 17.1 | 2.9 | 34.3 |
| others | 10 | 6 | 80.0 | 50.0 | 30.0 | 75.0 | 29.4 | 29.4 | 11.8 | 11.8 |
| all diagnoses | 393 | 139 | 61.3 | 38.1 | 28.2 | 12.2 | 25.0 | 9.6 | 3.8 | 21.4 |

* Complaints about both old and new employees.

significantly associated with diagnosis (p = 0.01). Complaints were more frequent among employees with a personality disorder diagnosis than among those diagnosed as psychotic (56 per cent as against 40 per cent). Only 25 per cent of alcoholics and addicts behaved oddly, fewer depressives (21 per cent) and fewer still neurotics (10 per cent).

It was also the handful of employees with a personality disorder diagnosis who attracted proportionately most complaints for disagreeable behaviour; then came the 'other' residual category, followed by addicts and alcoholics; 10 per cent or less of those diagnosed as psychotic, depressive, or neurotic were complained of for behaving in a disagreeable manner. Dangerous behaviour was shown to be a very rare event. Its incidence was notable only among psychotics (10 per cent) and among the residual 'other' category (12 per cent), the rate of occurrence among other diagnostic groups being less than 2 per cent.

Excessive sickness absence, commonly held to be a grave disadvantage to employers (Wansbrough 1974) was the subject of complaint only in one-fifth of all ex-patients. Diagnosis did not seem to affect this issue, but alcoholics and addicts attracted the highest number of complaints.

To summarize, the most frequently voiced complaints about ex-patients related to slowness, inadequacy, oddity, absence from work. The more dramatic extravagancy of conduct figured little, statistically. The psychotics of the C sample did not invariably score worse than otherwise diagnosed ex-patients. Depressives attracted complaints for slowness. Patients diagnosed as having a personality disorder evidently constituted tricky problems, but their numbers in one sample are too few for generalization. Neurotics, generally speaking, were seen to behave normally and work fast enough.

To be complained about is one thing. To lose a job on account of it is a graver matter altogether, and is an occurrence which varies slightly in the differing conditions of the different samples. A painstaking analysis was undertaken with a view to examining employers' tolerance of behaviour deviations in their employees. When does one get the sack? *Table 6(3)* illustrates the association of the three behaviour complaints with continued employment.

Statistical treatment of the subject can be supplemented by the story of an experiment reported some years ago, illustrating a variety of responses from different levels of an unusually benevolent management team. It also highlights the difficulties which can beset inexpert attempts at rehabilitation of the severely ill.

F. T. Ltd are motor component manufacturers. They count them-

Table 6(3)  (i) *The incidence of complaints about dangerous behaviour and its association with continued employment*

| sample | employee group | attracting complaints % | attracting complaints: % still employed | not attracting complaints: % still employed | sample size |
|---|---|---|---|---|---|
| Remploy | old | 7 | 33 | 74 | 45 |
| | new | 4 | 17 | 87 | 142 |
| Sample B | old | 7 | 75 | 84 | 54 |
| | new | 4 | 22 | 64 | 240 |
| Sample C | old | 5 | 72 | 89 | 398 |
| | new | 1 | 0 | 83 | 145 |

(ii) *The incidence of complaints about disagreeable behaviour and its association with continued employment*

| sample | employee group | attracting complaints % | attracting complaints: % still employed | not attracting complaints: % still employed | sample size |
|---|---|---|---|---|---|
| Remploy | old | 27 | 58 | 76 | 45 |
| | new | 16 | 69 | 97 | 142 |
| Sample B | old | 15 | 88 | 83 | 54 |
| | new | 10 | 52 | 63 | 240 |
| Sample C | old | 10 | 78 | 90 | 398 |
| | new | 7 | 60 | 84 | 145 |

(iii) *The incidence of complaints about odd behaviour and its association with continued employment*

| sample | employee group | attracting complaints % | attracting complaints: % still employed | not attracting complaints: % still employed | sample size |
|---|---|---|---|---|---|
| Remploy | old | 56 | 64 | 80 | 45 |
| | new | 30 | 81 | 85 | 142 |
| Sample B | old | 28 | 80 | 85 | 54 |
| | new | 24 | 47 | 67 | 240 |
| Sample C | old | 27 | 85 | 90 | 398 |
| | new | 19 | 70 | 85 | 145 |

selves as good employers (an opinion shared by the hospital employment officer they dealt with) and employ paraplegics and blind workers, exceeding their disablement quota. Many of their work people have been with the firm for many years. Mr E. G., supervisor of the assembly shops, had been there eighteen years, practically all his working life. The work is performed on a fast assembly line and the experience is that only some 50 per cent of all prospective employees, who are taken on a month's trial, are able to work up the necessary speed. But if Mr E. G. were obliged to fire an operator for being too slow, he could usually through his contacts find him or her another job, often in the factory over the road where the track was slower and no bonus was paid. Group and individual bonuses at F. T. brought the money well above the average for the area.

Clearly, as it stood F. T. represented an unsuitable milieu, one would have thought, for the rehabilitation of once severely ill workers, yet this was what the company had in mind. For a number of years work had been put out to a psychiatric rehabilitation workshop in the locality and as an experiment it was decided to accept a group of girls from there who were now judged ready for open employment. Eight girls started, four who had been living in hospital including one 'on a section' (i.e. a section of the Mental Health Act 1959 dealing with compulsory admission) and four trainees. They were put to work in complete isolation from the rest of the factory, packing various non-technical items at the going rate for the job. The whole project, from the first decisions to deal with the workshop in the first place, represented a humanitarian initiative on the part of F. T. management, as Mr A. A. S., the manufacturing manager, made clear. But sadly the scheme fell apart. The girls worked satisfactorily together for some two weeks and then bickering started. Absenteeism became a problem. Mr A. A. S.'s view was that the group 'fed on each other's problems' and that this was the main difficulty. The scheme lasted altogether something over two years, and when it came to an end the firm decided instead to engage individuals from time to time and try to integrate them into the whole factory.

Mr E. G., supervisor of the assembly shops, took up the story and first explained how Mr D. L., the girls' immediate supervisor, a man in his fifties, friendly and even-tempered, had been carefully chosen by management for the job. But the girls' disagreements got on even his nerves, and by the end, having become intensely involved with them and their troubles, he was under severe strain. Though the girls worked apart from the rest of the factory, they used the canteen, and most days Mr D. L. went with them. More specifically, two had a skirmish and one was asked to leave. Some were on medication, which they were meant to take themselves. Their output was slow and they never got to bonus standard. They seemed to be jealous of one another; only one was a reasonable operator. At one time, Mr E. G. tried to introduce a normal crew of operators facing them to try to make them pick up speed, but the girls never achieved a consistently fast working tempo. However, as has been explained, the firm only anticipated a 50 per cent success rate from normal new operators, so too much should not be made of the lack of speed.

Mr E. G. and the hospital employment officer together recalled the characteristics of members of the group. C. E. was 'a very domineering and meticulous type of person' who, when told to pack items four by four, refused to do so and insisted on packing them one by one, and what is more made the other girls pack them one by one also. This behaviour wore down Mr D. L.'s patience. She was eventually dismissed and sent back to hospital where after some time she went to work in the hospital library. There she remained happily for two years until she agreed to work in industry again, and was placed by the DRO on an inspection job in another firm. The managers at F. T. all agreed that inspection work suited her 'mentality'.

The views of Mr D. L., the immediate supervisor, were subsequently reported to the researcher in a letter from Mr A. A. S., manufacturing manager. He wrote:

'Contrary to my own personal feeling, Mr D. L. felt that keeping these people in a small group worked well and that, providing the group was always something in the order of 6–8 people, the atmosphere remained good, and, from the point of view of the supervisor concerned, produced a non-tension atmosphere in which he could communicate to them the needs of the job and induce a sufficiency of "small talk" amongst them that appeared to be necessary to maintain the atmosphere. There appeared to be a readiness, under gentle stimulation from Mr D. L. to talk freely about their particular problems including the reason for their "illness". Mr D. L. found them very receptive to instructions and encountered little or no resentment on this issue. Their activity in this section included packing and filling of bottles, which required some association with simple and quiet machinery; his opinion was that should it have been noisy machinery, such as a press, this would not have been acceptable to them.

The quality of their work was first class; here Mr D. L. felt that they should not be subjected to direct piece-work system, but they would react favourably to having targets set; again under gentle pressure they could be persuaded to hit these targets, although it would appear that their ability to maintain concentration and interest at this point was relatively short-lived, probably only for an hour at a time.

Mr D. L. did make the point that when the numbers involved reduced to two, a friction problem arose which caused him to confirm his viewpoint that 6–8 was a good size.

Although I have known Mr D. L. for many years, and selected him for this job because of his particular approach to people, I was staggered to find just how far his interest in these people went beyond the job. He told me that in times of sickness he visited them in hospital, and I learned from him that, of the eight people we had with us, five appear to be living a fairly normal life in that one has re-married, one is a librarian and three work in the locality in retail establishments.

I felt that you would be interested in a first-hand approach to the situation as portrayed by Mr D. L. 's comments to me. I think that without doubt any success we may have had stems from the fact that he personally became involved in the experiment. I cannot stress too much at this stage that the demand on the immediate supervisor is such that unless he is in the mould of Mr D. L. and sees this as complete involvement, then this type of operation could be most disappointing.'

This gallant but unhappily unsuccessful episode illustrates the differing responses of Messrs A. A. S., E. G., and D. L., who all none the less exhibited an unusual degree of benevolence towards their prospective rehabilitees. Mr A. A. S., the senior executive, clearly sensed the inadvisability of keeping the group too closely concentrated. Also, he was concerned to justify management's choice of Mr D. L. as supervisor, extolling his virtues and applauding his total identification with his charges. On the contrary Mr E. G., the middle-management man, believed that Mr D. L. had become overinvolved and tried to inculcate a semblance of normality into the scene by inducing a proper industrial tempo. The unfortunate Mr D. L. himself (who, it transpired, was simultaneously moving house and attempting to learn a new job against the demise of his existing one) was clearly doing his best, and was prepared to put up with a great deal until the obsessional one-by-one packer proved too provoking even for him. This story has been selected because of the company's shining good will: other firms would never for one moment have contemplated a similar disruption and predictable reactions of scepticism and disinterest would have done nothing to advance knowledge of the subject (Wansbrough (1971).)

## Employers' tolerance and available support

Are employers' attitudes to ex-patients influenced by the support available to them? Time and again in the research there cropped up the question of the extent and nature of the support needed by an ex-patient employee, and in fact also by his lay employer. In a previous chapter, the role of professional supporters was examined statistically, and it seemed as if firms deploying a full welfare staff proved to be no better as working milieux than others. On the other hand, contact with individual medical and nursing officers provided clear evidence, impossible to measure by statistical means, of the help and counsel so often proffered in a broad therapeutic relationship. Had this not been so, the monitoring of the Sample D subjects could never have been attempted.

We have not yet discussed the important area where the continuing support of the parent hospital seems to influence appreciably the attitudes of employers who may be persuaded to offer a chance to newcomers. The impression remains that small employers appreciate and even demand this life line, sensing that they do not know enough to be left on their own.

The first example that springs to mind was encountered in a northern city. A charge-nurse entrusted with the task of industrial liaison had enlisted the assistance of numerous employers, in industry and elsewhere, in providing opportunities for long-stay patients. One scheme, which could be regarded as a forerunner of an enclave, had been set up by him in a cutlery firm. A group of twelve female patients used to come by bus, 'on contract' to work in the factory. After a time, if they succeeded, they were taken on to the payroll as open workers. To clinch the deal, which took much hard bargaining with a hard-headed businessman, the charge-nurse, Mr W., had added a free supervisor in the shape of a nurse. This nurse was often in fact only a student nurse, but her uniformed presence reassured management, supervision, and work-people, not to mention the workers in the scheme. On the few occasions when a nurse had been absent, there had been trouble.

This same indomitable liaison officer had also secured a number of individual placements, some of which were seen in the course of a visit. It was fascinating to observe the extrovert methods employed by Mr W., who would charge into a factory and without hesitation go up to one of his ex-patients to ask him how he was, although Mr W. admitted that some of them did not appreciate this approach, among them a highly intelligent man who had returned to a foreman's job. Mr W. acknowledged that he often wondered whether he was on the right lines by emphasizing to the extent he did how patients and employers could rely on him personally, and whether this did not mean he was setting himself up too much as a father figure. The researcher can only comment that it worked, no doubt because of the personality of Mr W. Other individuals may succeed in providing the necessary support by less flamboyant means, and woe betide the day when anyone should endeavour to dictate which method is employed.

In fact the second example, in the South-West Midlands, is provided by a less extrovert character holding a similar position, who also commanded an extraordinary degree of collaboration among employers in the neighbourhood of the hospital. 'I would always take anyone from Mr L.' the researcher was told by one of these employers. The reason was that Mr L. and his staff made it their business to monitor their placements so long as they felt this necessary, making it plain that they would not leave employers in the lurch. No doubt other hospitals could provide similar instances. Could social service departments say the same?

Immediately accessible professional support is one of the key features of the enclave system whereby sheltered working groups of (Section II) severely disabled people work in a 'normal and undifferentiated' open setting instead of in a bricks and mortar sheltered workshop. At Bristol, Dr Early provided nurse supervision of the groups of sheltered workers in W. D. and H. O. Wills and Hygienic Straw (as it was first called). It was when the groups in other factories became rather small, one or two workers each to be precise, that the continuous presence of a nurse supervisor had to be diluted to a peripatetic weekly visit – still undertaken, be it noted, by a nurse. In our own experimental enclave project in the Southampton area, the key individual in the whole scheme was the nurse-trained special supervisor, peripatetic to a high degree among no less than eight employers at a time. At Croydon, it is true that the supervision of the enclave is now no longer provided by a nurse but by one of the firm's forewomen, known to the enclave workers for the greater part of its eight years' operation. In the present climate of ignorance, a professional presence clearly conveys reassurance when there is question of introducing, as newcomers, severely disabled workers either to sheltered enclaves or open employment.

# 7

# Absence from work

## The employer's attitude to absence

The dividing line between sickness absence and absenteeism is a blurred one. Sickness absence certified by a medical practitioner can be easily delineated, but the distinction between short-term (less than three working days), self-certified absence, and absenteeism is much less clear. Employers endeavour to discourage all absence and in particular short term absence by offering no sick pay over and above that available from the National Insurance Scheme, during the early months of an employee's service. None the less it has been observed that the frequency of sickness absence though not its magnitude decreases with an employee's length of service (Pocock 1973) and that there has been a rising trend in absence in all groups since the early 1960s (Whitehead 1971).

In employing the lately mentally ill we have found (Wansbrough and Cooper 1977) that one of the employers' main complaints is of excessive sickness absence. This misgiving is only surpassed by complaints about odd behaviour and is as frequent as complaints about slow work.

## A prospective study of sickness absence patterns

The 1975–6 study of 180 ex-patients in fifty-nine firms (Study D) provided for sickness absence of all durations to be recorded on a monthly basis by attributed cause of sickness for all ex-patients and a set of matched controls from the same firm. In five cases the sex of patients and controls was incorrectly matched and these cases are excluded from subsequent comparisons. An age match within ten years was achieved in all but twelve (7 per cent) of the remaining 175 cases. A successful match of occupation to the same major CODOT (Classification of Occupations and Directory of Trades) category was achieved in 162 (93 per cent) of cases. The major exceptions were the matching of ex-patients in the catering trades and the transport operating category. Length of service with the current employer however was not well matched: a match within two years was achieved only in 76 (43 per cent) of cases, the tendency being to match long-service patients with shorter service controls. This may tend to accentuate any difference observed, given the previously mentioned finding of Pocock (1973) that shorter service employees tend to experience lighter sickness absence than those with longer service.

Sickness absence was attributed to one of five categories: psychiatric sickness necessitating hospital admission, psychiatric sickness lasting more than three working days, other certified sickness, short term (less than three working days) or uncertified sickness, and absence for which none of these explanations was offered or apparent.

*Table 7(1)* shows the incidence and severity of different categories of sickness in the matched groups. 83 per cent of ex-patients are absent

Table 7(1)  *Fifty-nine companies 1975–6; 180 subjects and matched controls: all sickness absence*

| | | | for those falling sick | |
| category of sickness | group | proportion falling sick | average annual absence – working days | average annual absence – spells |
| --- | --- | --- | --- | --- |
| psychiatric hospital | subjects | 0.12 (0.02) | 26.6 (5.2) | 1.9 (0.2) |
| admission | controls | 0.01 (0.01) | 20.8 ( — ) | 1.7 ( — ) |
| certified non- | subjects | 0.47 (0.04) | 22.3 (3.0) | 2.2 (0.2) |
| psychiatric sickness | controls | 0.41 (0.04) | 17.9 (3.4) | 1.8 (0.1) |
| certified psychiatric | subjects | 0.26 (0.03) | 42.0 (6.5) | 2.6 (0.3) |
| sickness | controls | 0.01 (0.01) | 2.8 ( — ) | 1.7 ( — ) |
| uncertified (short- | subjects | 0.58 (0.04) | 4.6 (0.6) | 3.4 (0.4) |
| term sickness | controls | 0.37 (0.04) | 3.3 (0.5) | 2.3 (0.3) |
| unexplained absence | subjects | 0.21 (0.03) | 4.1 (0.9) | 2.6 (0.6) |
| | controls | 0.12 (0.02) | 3.6 (0.8) | 3.4 (0.8) |
| all categories | subjects | 0.83 (0.03) | 34.2 (4.0) | 5.3 (0.4) |
| of sickness | controls | 0.60 (0.04) | 14.9 (2.4) | 3.4 (0.3) |

*Note*: Proportions total more than 1, as one subject may experience sickness absence in more than one category during the year.
Bracketed figures are the estimated standard errors (where these are computable) of the preceding statistic.

during a year as opposed to 60 per cent of the matched control group. The sickness absence of ex-patients is more extensive than that of the controls, average total annual absence being thirty-four as opposed to fifteen working days comprising an average 5.3 as opposed to 3.4 spells of absence per annum. The excesses of the ex-patients' sickness absence arise in several categories of sickness. 12 per cent of ex-patients are readmitted to hospital whilst some 26 per cent experience a recurrence of some form of psychiatric illness. Apart from this, the characteristics of their certified sickness absence differ little from those of the control group. The severity of the short term and unexplained absence of the ex-patients is not much greater than that of the controls, but the percentages of ex-patients experiencing these categories of absence are markedly greater; 58 per cent as opposed to 37 per cent having some short term absence and 21 per cent as opposed to 12 per cent having some unexplained absence.

Thus, if we discount recurrences of psychiatric problems, it is the proportion of former in-patients falling sick which is higher than that for the control group, rather than there being any marked differences in the annual length of absence or the annual number of spells of absence.

We have so far distinguished between different categories of absence; but this is not normally what causes an employer most concern. His interest is in total absence and in particular, total certified absence (our first three categories). We shall first examine the characteristics of total absence.

It is known that sickness absence varies with age and sex. The 'classical' analysis (Benjamin and Haycocks 1971) is to produce a set of rates in working days per year exposed-to-risk by age and sex. However, it is possible to break down these rates into three components and to examine these with a view to gaining more insight into the nature of sickness absence. The breakdown takes the following form:

$$\frac{\text{total working days of sickness}}{\text{total years of exposed to risk (generating the sickness)}} = \frac{\text{years of exposed to risk with sickness}}{\text{total years of exposed to risk}} \times \frac{\text{total spells of sickness}}{\text{years of exposed to risk with sickness}} \times \frac{\text{total working days of sickness}}{\text{total spells of sickness}}$$

which may be expressed as:

sickness rate = proportion × mean number of spells × mean length
falling sick      of those falling sick      of spell

or symbolically:

$$S_x = P_x.\mathcal{N}_x.L_x$$

Sometimes a breakdown into two components: $P_x.\mathcal{N}_x$ and $L_x$ is used. The product $P_x.\mathcal{N}_x$ is then termed the inception rate.

The matching of subjects and controls allows us to make valid comparison between the groups; however the small size of the study (a maximum of 180 years exposed to risk) means that the resulting sampling errors will be large.

*Table 7(2)* gives details for the sample of men by age. The sickness rates of former patients (working days per man year exposed to the risk of sickness) are much worse than the control group at all ages. A larger proportion of the psychiatric group can be expected to fall sick, 87 per cent as opposed to 59 per cent; those who fall sick will have more spells of sickness, an average of 5.0 spells as opposed to 2.9 spells per annum; however the duration of these spells will only be slightly longer than those of the control group, an average of 6.8 compared to 5.8 working days. This inflation in the number and length of spells is mainly the result of a recurrence of psychiatric problems as we have already seen.

*Table 7(3)* gives the results for the sample of women by age. Their experience is remarkably similar to that of men. A large proportion of the psychiatric group fall sick during a year, 86 per cent compared to 69 per cent; the frequency of sickness amongst those falling sick is high, an average of 5.9 spells as opposed to 4.3 spells per annum; and each of these spells is longer for the psychiatric group, 4.4 working days compared to 2.4 working days on average.

### A comparison of certified sickness absence amongst different groups

As remarked earlier, an employer's main concern is with certified absence. Repeated short-term absenteeism may be trying, but as a problem this is by no means confined to ex-patients.

Data collected in a large manufacturing company over the period 1966–74 enable us to make some useful comparisons between former in-patients, a sample of employees who had experienced coronary disease, and a control group taken from the workforce at large. The first group consisted of fifty-four men who, whilst in the employ of the company, had received psychiatric hospital in-patient treatment and had then returned to employment. Some had returned to their old employment

Table 7(2)  *Fifty-nine companies 1975–6; 135 men and matched controls: all sickness absence*

| | psychiatric group | | | | | control group | | | | |
| | exposed to risk | $P_x$ | $N_x$ | $L_x$ | $S_x$ | exposed to risk | $P_x$ | $N_x$ | $L_x$ | $S_x$ |
| age, x | | | | | | | | | | |
|---|---|---|---|---|---|---|---|---|---|---|
| 15–24 | 5.0 | 1.00 | 6.6 | 2.7 | 17.6 (8.7) | 7.6 | 0.73 | 6.3 | 1.5 | 7.0 (2.4) |
| 25–34 | 4.6 | 1.00 | 8.1 | 3.8 | 30.2 (16.5) | 3.0 | 0.67 | 2.0 | 6.3 | 8.3 (4.8) |
| 35–44 | 7.5 | 0.58 | 2.5 | 6.2 | 9.1 (8.0) | 4.2 | 0.48 | 4.0 | 4.0 | 7.7 (6.7) |
| 45–54 | 17.1 | 0.88 | 6.3 | 3.9 | 21.7 (5.4) | 16.4 | 0.79 | 4.6 | 2.3 | 8.3 (2.7) |
| 55–59 | 3.0 | 1.00 | 3.7 | 13.7 | 50.2 (16.5) | 6.0 | 0.50 | 1.3 | 5.2 | 3.5 (1.7) |
| 15–59 | 37.2 | 0.86 | 5.9 | 4.4 | 21.9 (4.1) | 37.2 | 0.69 | 4.3 | 2.4 | 7.2 (1.5) |

*Note:* Estimated standard errors of rates are given in brackets.

Table 7(3)  *Fifty-nine companies 1975–6; forty women and matched controls: all sickness absence*

| age, x | psychiatric group | | | | | control group | | | | |
|---|---|---|---|---|---|---|---|---|---|---|
| | exposed to risk | $P_x$ | $N_x$ | $L_x$ | $S_x$ | exposed to risk | $P_x$ | $N_x$ | $L_x$ | $S_x$ |
| 15–24 | 5.0 | 1.00 | 6.6 | 2.7 | 17.6 (8.7) | 7.6 | 0.73 | 6.3 | 1.5 | 7.0 (2.4) |
| 25–34 | 4.6 | 1.00 | 8.1 | 3.8 | 30.2 (16.5) | 3.0 | 0.67 | 2.0 | 6.3 | 8.3 (4.8) |
| 35–44 | 7.7 | 0.58 | 2.5 | 6.2 | 9.1 (8.0) | 4.2 | 0.48 | 4.0 | 4.0 | 7.7 (6.7) |
| 45–54 | 17.1 | 0.88 | 6.3 | 3.9 | 21.7 (5.4) | 16.4 | 0.79 | 4.6 | 2.3 | 8.3 (2.7) |
| 55–59 | 3.0 | 1.00 | 3.7 | 13.7 | 50.2 (16.5) | 6.0 | 0.50 | 1.3 | 5.2 | 3.5 (1.7) |
| 15–59 | 37.2 | 0.86 | 5.9 | 4.4 | 21.9 (4.1) | 37.2 | 0.69 | 4.3 | 2.4 | 7.2 (1.5) |

*Note*: Estimated standard errors of rates are given in brackets.

but the majority were working in a specially equipped workshop undertaking simple repetitive tasks. The second group contained seventy-one men who at some stage had suffered from coronary disease, twenty-three of them dying during the observation period. In the main these subjects were treated as normal healthy workers in respect of job placement. The third group was a randomly chosen sample of ninety-two men from the company workforce.

This study within the single company has the advantage of a large number of years exposed to the risk of sickness – resulting in smaller sampling errors of the estimates; however, the samples from the coronary and control groups have not been matched with the psychiatric group. Thus we must be cautious in making comparisons between the groups. Looking at the overall sickness rates, $S_x$ ( *Table 7(4)* ), for the psychiatric and the coronary groups we can see that there

Table 7(4)   *Manufacturing industry 1966–74: certified sickness absence*

| Age, x | psychiatric (54 men) | | | | |
| | exposed to risk | $P_x$ | $N_x$ | $L_x$ | $S_x$ |
| --- | --- | --- | --- | --- | --- |
| 16–30 | 74.0 | 0.66 | 2.7 | 15.4 | 27.4 |
| 31–40 | 161.5 | 0.65 | 2.2 | 14.5 | 20.9 |
| 41–50 | 119.0 | 0.46 | 1.7 | 14.1 | 10.7 |
| 51–64 | 76.5 | 0.56 | 2.6 | 11.6 | 16.9 |
| 16–64 | 431.0 | 0.58 | 2.2 | 14.1 | 18.5 |

| Age, x | coronary (71 men) | | | | |
| | exposed to risk | $P_x$ | $N_x$ | $L_x$ | $S_x$ |
| --- | --- | --- | --- | --- | --- |
| 16–30 | – | – | – | – | – |
| 31–40 | 21.0 | 0.42 | 1.1 | 21.7 | 10.4 |
| 41–50 | 128.5 | 0.38 | 1.8 | 24.4 | 15.6 |
| 51–64 | 272.5 | 0.38 | 1.9 | 35.1 | 25.3 |
| 16–64 | 422.0 | 0.41 | 1.7 | 32.2 | 22.1 |

| Age, x | control (92 men) | | | | |
| | exposed to risk | $P_x$ | $N_x$ | $L_x$ | $S_x$ |
| --- | --- | --- | --- | --- | --- |
| 16–30 | 197.0 | 0.19 | 1.8 | 7.2 | 2.5 |
| 31–40 | 229.5 | 0.27 | 1.4 | 10.8 | 4.2 |
| 41–50 | 143.0 | 0.31 | 1.5 | 18.9 | 8.8 |
| 51–64 | 93.5 | 0.21 | 1.3 | 11.4 | 3.1 |
| 16–64 | 663.0 | 0.25 | 1.5 | 12.1 | 4.5 |

is little to choose between them, but they both definitely experience much higher rates of absence than the workforce at large in the factory.

Whilst the psychiatric and the coronary group overall rates by age are similar, the characteristics of absence are different. 55–65 per cent of the psychiatric group will fall sick in any year, having an average two or three spells of sickness, each lasting for an expected twelve to fifteen working days. In the coronary group only 35–45 per cent will fall sick in any year, having an average one to two spells of sickness, but each lasting for an expected twenty-five to thirty-five working days.

These characteristics can be compared with those of the control group within the same factory, of whom 20–30 per cent fall sick per year, averaging one to two spells of sickness, each lasting for about ten to fifteen working days. We might summarize the situation of the former psychiatric patients in this company as more likely to fall sick more often, but with each spell of sickness being no longer than those of the average employee. This pattern is similar to that observed for certified sickness absence for men in the control group of the 1975–6 study: about 30–40 per cent falling sick each year having an average of one to two spells of sickness, each lasting about eight to ten working days.

This is a well established pattern and is confirmed by larger scale studies. The General Household Survey of 1973 estimated a rate of 9.1 working days for all sickness. There were large variations across occupational groups; absence was lowest in the professional classes at 3.9 working days, and highest in the unskilled groups at 18.4 working days. Manual workers had higher rates of absence than non-manual workers. The majority of ex-patients employees studied are in semi-skilled and unskilled occupations. A critical appraisal of the National Insurance Statistics for 1973 (Taylor 1974) suggests that the rate for certified sickness absence is about ten working days.

These tentative results lead us to conclude that former psychiatric patients do experience more sickness absence than an average employee; however, it is little worse than at least one chronic condition, namely coronary disease.

The excesses of absence loom large in an employer's eyes because of the patterns of absences. Whereas in the coronary group there are no younger people, in the ex-patient group a large proportion are absent from every age group. The employer tends to gain the superficial impression that they are 'always away sick'.

## Other factors associated with absence

The pattern of variation of absence by age and sex has been examined in some detail. This variation is to be expected amongst all employees, although as we have seen the patterns of variation may differ between different sub-groups. The data from Study D allows us to look more closely at the variation in absence patterns for former in-patients. Even when an allowance is made for the effects of age and sex there still remains variation between the absence record of employees.

The length of the previous cumulative stay in a psychiatric hospital is positively associated with the number of spells of psychiatric sickness absence experienced during the year of observation. The effect is most pronounced at the extremes of the distribution of stay. Those with a cumulative stay of less than three months have an average of 0.4 spells per year and those with a previous hospital stay of more than five years experience an average of 1.5 spells per year, whilst between these extremes the average is about 0.8 spells per year. After allowing for the effects of age and sex the length of previous hospital stays is not associated with the total amount of psychiatric sickness in a year, thus the differences observed in the over five years group seem to arise from more frequent spells of psychiatric sickness, which are each of shorter duration than the average spell. The length of previous stay is not associated with the frequency and amount of certified non-psychiatric or short-term sickness absence after allowing for the effects of age and sex.

Psychiatric diagnosis is associated with the frequency of psychiatric sickness and also with the amount of short-term sickness after allowing for the effects of age and sex. Those diagnosed as reactive depressive have an average of 0.5 spells of psychiatric sickness per year compared to an overall average of about 1.0 spell per year for other diagnoses. The same diagnostic group has an average of 6.3 working days of short term absence per year compared to an average of 2.7 working days per year for the other diagnostic groups. This excess arises from longer but not more frequent short-term absences amongst those diagnosed as reactive depressive.

The duration of an employee's current employment is negatively associated with many features of the sickness absence record. This is a phenomenon which has been observed in many other situations (Pocock 1973) and is often attributed to the operation of eligibility rules for a company sick-pay scheme. In this study it is the frequency rather than the amount of the various categories of absence which exhibits these patterns. The frequency of psychiatric sickness falls markedly after ten years service. The average is 0.6 spells per year after ten years' service compared to 1.2 spells per year for shorter durations of employment. The frequency of non-psychiatric certified sickness has a similar pattern; 0.9 spells per year after ten years service compared to an average of 1.2 spells per year for shorter durations. The same features are apparent in the records of the frequency of short term absence; an average of 1.8 spells per year after ten years' service compared to 3.1 spells per year for shorter durations. These differences remain even after allowing for the effects of age and sex.

The most striking patterns remaining after allowing for age and sex are in relation to the time since the former patient's last discharge from hospital. All the Study D data was collected during 1976, thus the calendar year of last discharge provides a suitable proxy for time since last discharge from hospital. The frequency and amount of certified psychiatric sickness is much higher within about four years of last discharge than it is after this time (*Table 7(5)*). This pattern persists after allowance is made for the effect of age and sex. The relationships between the amount and frequency of certified absence and time since last discharge are more complicated. Before the removal of the effects of age and sex the trends are not very pronounced (*Table 7(5)*); after their removal earlier calendar years (pre 1970) have more frequent spells with a smaller average amount of certified sickness per year than the later calendar years, where the average amount is larger but the frequency is smaller. Thus in the early years following discharge the pattern is of infrequent long spells of certified absence changing in the later years to more frequent short spells of certified absence. The trends for short-term sickness also become more pronounced, when we allow for the effects of age and sex. In the early years following the last discharge there are very frequent, slightly longer spells than in the later years when the frequency of spells decreases but their average length drops only slightly.

## Implications for the employment
## of former in-patients

Our studies have established the characteristics of the absence patterns of former in-patients by age and sex. The general impression of employers that the absence is higher than that amongst the work force at large is confirmed. However, such excesses are not confined to the psychiatrically disabled and can equally be found in those suffering from chronic physical conditions. Even amongst the psychiatrically disabled there are those who do not experience excessive sickness

Table 7(5)  *Frequency and amount of sickness absence by cause and calendar year of last hospital discharge*

| calendar year of hospital discharge | sample size | certified psychiatric sickness | | certified non-psychiatric sickness | | short-term sickness: all causes | |
|---|---|---|---|---|---|---|---|
| | | spells per year | working days per year | spells per year | working days per year | spells per year | working days per year |
| 1965 | 2 | 0.5 | 3.2 | 1.5 | 11.4 | 0.5 | 2.5 |
| 1966 | 4 | 0.5 | 6.3 | 1.5 | 7.0 | 2.8 | 2.9 |
| 1967 | 8 | 0.1 | 2.5 | 0.5 | 5.5 | 0.8 | 1.0 |
| 1968 | 7 | 0 | 0 | 0.7 | 10.0 | 2.6 | 3.0 |
| 1969 | 8 | 0 | 0 | 1.4 | 12.0 | 2.4 | 2.5 |
| 1970 | 7 | 0.1 | 0.7 | 1.1 | 6.7 | 1.9 | 1.6 |
| 1971 | 11 | 1.2 | 32.3 | 1.3 | 17.6 | 4.1 | 12.9 |
| 1972 | 21 | 1.6 | 23.1 | 0.9 | 5.0 | 2.2 | 3.1 |
| 1973 | 24 | 0.6 | 14.3 | 1.5 | 19.0 | 3.0 | 3.0 |
| 1974 | 60 | 1.1 | 17.3 | 1.1 | 8.5 | 2.6 | 2.5 |
| 1975 | 8 | 1.4 | 29.3 | 0.6 | 22.5 | 1.1 | 1.2 |

*Source:* Study D

absence. However, rehabilitation measured by the sickness absence criteria takes several years, rather than months, to achieve following discharge from hospital. An employer's misgivings with respect to excessive absence during this rehabilitation period can be alleviated somewhat if he knows what to expect. Hopefully, we have made a start in describing what might be expected. Further studies which confirm the age/sex patterns of absence and determine more precisely the length and course of the rehabilitation period following hospital discharge are needed.

# 8

## Relapse

### The employer's attitude to relapse

Twenty years ago, Olshansky (1958) and his colleagues in Massachusetts listed the matters perceived by employers as constituting difficulty when hiring the ex-mental patient: concern with possible violence; a low tolerance threshold of pressure and speed; 'incompatibility'; bizarre behaviour; a need for close supervision; and, a very prominent concern, fear of a recurrence of illness or relapse. Analysis of the comments of our own occupational health doctor respondents identified very much the same matters: a tendency towards excessive sickness absence; disturbance of the work of others; difficulties of personal relationship; and again, a recurrence of illness or relapse. Episodes of extreme oddity of behaviour or of acute breakdown leading to violence, feared by the earlier employers, had however been found to affect only a small minority (Wansbrough 1974).

The possibility of a relapse is always present. This is what makes an ex-patient 'chronic' in the same way as a chronically physically ill employee. Even after five years of apparent complete normality relapses were reported in the case-study firm which took on a batch of one hundred ex-patients from a psychiatric hospital (Wansbrough 1973). Enlightened employers are always aware of the higher risk in the early years and are prepared to tolerate in the ensuing years a risk no greater than that attached to other misfortunes which can befall any employee. But there is no way this risk can be reduced to zero.

These statements can be made despite the advances recorded in detecting 'triggering' events, for it may be years before these discoveries can be turned to practical account on the employment scene. Not only is the risk of relapse always present, but more than one doctor thought that the relapse rate was tending to increase as patients were discharged into community care after the shorter hospital stays outlined in Chapter 2. Indeed, it may be said that the rate of increase will measure the success of the policy of emptying the hospitals.

For anyone with a psychiatric history to suffer a relapse is a disaster of greater or lesser proportions, even though he be elderly and retired or living a quiet life at home. But a relapse at work can mean that a man's job is at stake together with all the years of careful rehabilitation which have got him there. Many employers are prepared to act to safeguard this investment.

### Recognizing a possible relapse

One of the biggest problems is to detect the onset of a relapse in good time and get the ex-patient back for treatment. One doctor wrote: 'I rely on the foreman to let us know when this is beginning to recur – we always try and give the foreman the likely symptoms of a relapse when a new patient is taken on – just as one gives the foreman the symptoms of a diabetic.' This seems sensible, for it is his supervisor and work-mates who are in daily contact with the ex-patient, not the doctor in his surgery who may be easily misled in a short interview. To involve the foreman, however, is sometimes seen as a breach of medical confidentiality. In order to test the extent to which secrecy is maintained, and correspondingly, the extent to which foremen and others are involved, information was collected in the 1973 survey. It was found in the open employment Sample C I, that 85 per cent of management alone, or management and workers, were told about the illness of an employee returning to work after in-patient psychiatric treatment. This represented 87 per cent in the case of psychotics, and 85 per cent in the case of depressives and neurotics.

If the supervisor is to be involved in the detection of impending relapse, what should he look out for? The records of Study D provide examples: lack of concentration, deterioration and unevenness of work standards, wandering away from the place of work, disagreeable behaviour to work mates, carelessness in personal hygiene and appearance are all indicators remarked by the record-keepers in this study, as well as the detachment and withdrawal which are perhaps beginning to be more generally understood. The prospective monthly records were therefore analysed with a view to defining the characteristics of behaviour in employees who relapsed as compared to those who did not relapse.

Table 8(1)  *Who at work is told of an employee's psychiatric illness on return to work. Percentages, by diagnosis, Sample C I*

| | psychoses (n = 70) | all depressions (n = 222) | neuroses (n = 54) | personality disorders (n = 7) | alcoholism and addiction (n = 22) | organic and other (n = 10) | total (n = 385) |
|---|---|---|---|---|---|---|---|
| management told | 56 | 62 | 61 | 29 | 64 | 40 | 60 |
| workers told | 0 | 1 | 2 | 0 | 9 | 0 | 1 |
| management and workers told | 31 | 22 | 22 | 29 | 18 | 40 | 24 |
| nobody told | 13 | 16 | 15 | 42 | 9 | 20 | 15 |

*Source*: The Employer's Standpoint. Unpublished Report to Department of Health and Social Security, 1974.

## Patterns of performance and behaviour at work

There have been several attempts to measure performance and behaviour at work. Earlier studies (Cheadle *et al*. 1967; Griffiths 1973) were concerned with the assessment of aspects of behaviour in sheltered work situations with a view to predicting which ex-patients would make good employees. Cheadle *et al*. used a series of questions to supervisors in Employment Rehabilitation Centres about the performance of ex-patients (see Appendix 2) utilizing the questionnaire devised by Dr Roger Morgan. Griffiths used a revised and expanded version of this report form for assessment in a rehabilitation workshop attached to the Maudsley Hospital (Appendix 2). Both questionnaires used the concept of an 'average performance' against which the current abilities of the ex-patient were to be judged. In the case of the Morgan Work Report average performance was that of ex-patients in general. Griffiths worked with supervisors having industrial experience and an average performance was deemed to be that of an employee undertaking a similar task in open employment.

The monthly report form used in the present prospective study (Study D) is similar to that used by Griffiths in that the concept of average remains the same. However our subjects are in open employment and our respondents are medical staff who are collecting information about work performance and behaviour at one stage removed from direct and continuous observation. Thus some of the items in the Griffiths questionnaire were not appropriate to the current study. The relevant part of the questionnaire used is displayed in Appendix 2.

Both Cheadle and Griffiths collected information at a single point in time with the object of predicting future satisfactory employment. Griffiths subjected data for thirty subjects, with twenty-five items recorded for each, to a principal component analysis. The analysis identified five clusters of items which Griffiths (1977) argued reflected the following employee characteristics: task competence, response to authority and supervision, relationships with others, work motivation and enthusiasm, confidence and initiative. The results show that any of these scores provides a useful predictor of future employability, the confidence and initiative factor being the most useful. None of the scores were related to patients' age nor to an index of their contact with the psychiatric services (length of time since the first of such contacts). The scores were largely independent of scores obtained on intelligence (WAIS) and personality (PEN and MMPI) tests.

Griffiths obtained his factor scores from a weighted sum of the patient's scores for each of the five identified groups of questions. For the majority of factors the principal component weights were almost equal. Therefore, in our own descriptive analysis of work records we have opted to weight responses to questions in each group equally. The factors identified, their components, the possible ranges of scores and their interpretation are given in *Table 8(2)*. The first three factors reflect different aspects of the employee's ability to carry out his allotted duties in terms of competence in, and consistency of, performance requiring no more than the accepted degree of supervision. The remaining two factors attempt to evaluate the social adjustment of the employee in terms of his acceptance by his colleagues and his reactions to colleagues and supervisors in the work situation. This dichotomy corresponds to that which Bennett (1975) has termed the 'task' and 'role' characteristics of a job.

Table 8(2)     *Items included in each of the five factors*

---

(1) Task competence
standard of work
speed of work
ability to cope with instructions
(Three items: score range 3–15. High scores indicate poor performance)

(2) Task consistency
variation in the quality of work from day to day
(One item: score range 1–2. Low scores indicate poor performance)

(3) Supervision required
how much supervision required compared to others doing similar work
(One item: score range 1–5. High scores indicate poor performance)

(4) Relationship with others
influence in the work of others
how others related to him
control of emotions
(Three items: score range 3–16. High scores indicate poor performance)

(5) Confidence and response to authority
social relationship with others
acceptance of authority
(Two items: score range 2–10)

---

Prospective records over one year were collected for 123 former in-patients. This group consisted of ninety-four males and twenty-nine females; twenty-five psychotics, twenty-four neurotics, nineteen re-active depressives, forty 'other' depressives and fifteen with other diagnoses. The patterns of behaviour as exhibited by the five factors described are markedly different for those who experienced some relapse during the year compared to those who did not experience any relapse. Seventeen subjects were admitted to hospital during the year and sixteen subjects were absent from work for psychiatric reasons on ten or more working days during the year. This group were classified as 'relapses', the remainder being classified as having not relapsed.

*Figure 8(1)* displays the average profile on the work competence factor for these two groups. The competence of the relapse group is in general below that of the 'average employee' and more variable than the non-relapse group, which is better than the 'average employee'. *Figure 8(2)* indicates in same fashion the consistency in the quality of the work of the two groups. Both groups have a proportion of subjects with a standard of work which fluctuates more than would be expected of the 'average employee'. However in the relapse group this proportion is much higher than in the non-relapse group and varies much more markedly from month to month. *Figure 8(4)* displays the averages scores over time for the amount of supervision required. All subjects required on average at least as much supervision as the 'average employee'. The amount required was reasonably constant over time with the relapse group requiring slightly more supervision.

Thus the evidence is that relapse is heralded by poorer standards of job performance and a marked variation in these standards over time – the deterioration and unevenness of work standards mentioned previously.

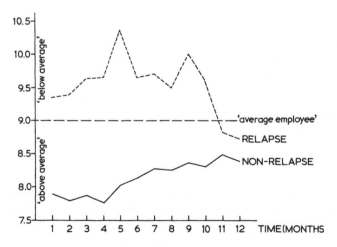

*Figure 8(1)*    Task competence factor profiles

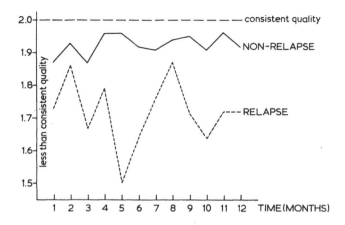

*Figure 8(2)*   Task consistency factor profiles

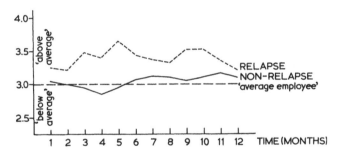

*Figure 8(3)*   Supervision required factor profiles

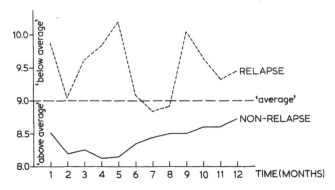

*Figure 8(4)*   Relationships with others factor profiles

*Figure 8(4)* displays the profiles reflecting the success of relationships with others. The pattern in the relapse group is of much more variability than in the non-relapse group and shows less successful interaction with others. The final factor *(Figure 8(5))* reflecting an amalgam of social confidence in relationships with others and response to authority shows little difference between the two groups. Overall it is the instability, as well as slightly inferior performance, both in the material and social aspects of being an employee which characterizes those who relapse.

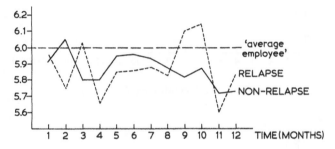

*Figure 8(5)* Confidence and response to authority profiles

## Events which might be construed as precipitating or 'triggering' relapses at work

Within the last eighteen years a great deal of work has been done by Brown and Wing and their colleagues at the Institute of Psychiatry on the influence of family and social factors on the onset of schizophrenic illness and relapse. Vaughn and Leff's replication includes depressed neurotics. While our larger sample consists not of a random sample from a cohort of discharged patients, but a selected group of working ex-patients, it is hoped that the information we provide may slot in to complete the overall picture.

Brown and Birley (1970) showed that crises and life changes precipitate the onset and relapse of acute schizophrenic states. For this study, fifty randomly selected patients were interviewed, together with at least one other informant, about the occurrence of certain previously defined and dateable events occurring either to themselves or to close relatives, within the three months prior to admission. These events, chosen on the basis of common sense, including moving house, admission to hospital, birth, marriage, or death, and starting or leaving a job. These were classified as 'independent' or 'possibly independent' of the patients' ability to influence them.

In the three weeks immediately prior to onset or relapse, twenty-three, or 46 per cent of the patients had experienced at least one 'independent' event, as compared to an average of 12 per cent of patients experiencing such an event in each of the three earlier three-week periods. A comparison group of 325 persons at their place of work were then interviewed in the same manner, and it was found that the percentage of those experiencing an event was constant over all four three-week periods. Unlike the patients, they underwent no increase in experiencing events in the last three-week period. The researchers concluded that there had been a real increase in the rate of events experienced by the patients which could not have been brought about by abnormal behaviour on their part, and which they see therefore as genuine, external, precipitating events. Brown and Birley looked also at the influence of drugs, finding that the stopping of phenothiazine did have an effect on the thirteen patients in their sample who did so.

A major source of crisis and life-change has been the family, an area of study which the anti-psychiatrists, headed by Laing, have got hold of and turned upside down, ending up with the contention that it is the family and not the patient which is mad. As so often, schizophrenia has been the chosen diagnosis. In a famous study (Brown *et al.* 1962) 128 schizophrenic men were followed up for one year after leaving hospital. 55 per cent deteriorated during the year, and it was found that patients returning to a relative who showed 'high emotional involvement' deteriorated more frequently than patients returning to a relative who showed 'low emotional involvement'. It was also found that the proportion of patients who deteriorated amongst those living in lodgings and those living with relatives was similar. The evidence seemed to be that an intermediate setting for living – not too much opportunity for over-involvement, not too much for complete social withdrawal – offered the best chance for survival.

The project was replicated ten years later with a more highly developed technique, the concept of 'high emotional involvement' on the part of relatives giving way to the more precise 'expressed emotion' measure, E.E. (Brown *et al.* 1972). The result was the same. A high degree of emotion expressed by relatives was found to be strongly associated with relapse during the nine months after discharge.

The evidence has been summarized by Wing in a lecture to the American College of Psychiatrists (1977):

'On the one hand, too much social stimulation, experienced by the patient as social intrusiveness, may lead to an acute relapse. On the other hand, too little stimulation will exacerbate any tendency already present towards social withdrawal, slowness, underactivity and an apparent lack of motivation. Thus the patient has to walk a tight-rope between two different types of danger, and it is easy to become decompensated either way.'

The above refers to relapses in schizophrenia. It was left to Vaughn and Leff (1976) to plug to some extent the gap in knowledge of this process in conditions other than schizophrenia. These two authors found that for depressed patients as for schizophrenics there was a significant link between key relatives' criticisms and relapse, but all in all, they considered the relapse pattern for depressed patients to be not the same as for schizophrenics, since they appeared even more vulnerable to criticism.

### Home-based and work-based triggering events

In order to supplement these studies by reference to our own Study D it was necessary, in addition to utilizing the coded data, to scrutinize the individual records. The sections examined were the record-keepers' open-ended comments on any problems or unusual disruptions of the work situation affecting the employee, and the answers to questions about changes in job, marital status or living circumstances. The records scrutinized numbered fifty-three.

Collecting data by using open ended questions does not ensure that all the relevant information will be recorded. However our respondents were very much aware of the importance of recording all changes in the circumstances of the individual subject, which had been noted either by medical staff or by the subject's foreman or supervisor.

Of the 180 subjects taking part in the prospective study fifty-three experienced a relapse of some kind. In investigating the circumstances surrounding these episodes we have divided these subjects into three groups; namely those admitted to a psychiatric hospital (numbering twenty), those not admitted to hospital but experiencing at least ten working days sickness absence attributed to psychiatric causes (numbering twenty-seven) and the final group of six, who were not admitted to hospital but experienced between one and ten working days' sickness due to psychiatric causes. From amongst each of these groups we will present some case histories which illustrate the division between home and work based 'triggering' events. This delineation is not clear in all cases.

The group of relapses which necessitated hospital admission yielded five cases which illustrate the triggering of relapse by home based events.

(a) An assistant accountant aged twenty-one, with five years' service, had first been admitted to hospital for forty-two days with depression before the record period began. One month later the record read: 'Reconciled with the young lady and her two children whom he gave up in August which then caused him to be an in-patient due to depression.' Four months later came the entry 'Still having girl friend problem', and one month later: 'His relationship which was dodgy with his common law wife seems settled at present.' The final entry to the effect that there appeared to be a dispute between his mother and his girl friend left us in doubt of the eventual outcome of his problem, but in little doubt that the triggering event, if any, was home rather than work-based.

(b) In a London hospital, a student nurse, who had already previously attempted suicide, was admitted to psychiatric ward. Her distress this time was attributed by the record-keeper to her break with her boy friend.

By the end of the record she had completed eight months' further training and 'made considerable overall improvement, having finally managed to sort out her personal relationships and being much the better for it'.

(c) A quality control inspector of forty-five, in hospital when the record started, had made progress there but had immediately deteriorated when he was discharged home. The record reported marital troubles, stating that this employee was much happier either in hospital, or staying with his sister, which he did for a while, than he was at home. The noise in the factory was also mentioned; as a contributory factor rather than the major cause of distress.

(d) Also apparently home based were the events preceding the admission of an engineering craftsman, a schizophrenic, who resigned of his own volition having decided that he needed full-time hospitalization. (He had already been sleeping in hospital.) 'He resigned from the company against the firm advice of the Personnel Department but was promised his job back if he so wished on his discharge from hospital.' It then became known that he and his wife had separated.

(e) The picture concerning a meter-reader of forty is less clear. He was reported as being affected by the pressure of work before the Christmas holiday and was absent for two months certified psychiatric sickness. However, it was the first anniversary of his father's death which preceded his hospital admission.

Within the same group we have identified four cases where the triggering event is to be found in the working situation.

(a)  A thirty-two year old male factory process worker of eleven years' service diagnosed as depressive was working for four months without apparent difficulty, but was then absent for two months, one of them in hospital. Three months earlier, a job change appeared in the record, though whether entailing greater or less responsibility we cannot assess. He remained in the same department. One month after his return to work he was reported as having coped with increased pressure very successfully. Two months later: 'Because of increased work, 4 extra men were sent to his section, which seemed to upset him and he went on sick leave'. He was still away a month later.

There seems little doubt that the arrival of the four extra men was responsible for his latest absence, a point of some interest in view of his having been reported as coping successfully with the pressure two months earlier.

His previous change of job evoked no comment from the record-keeper. It could have acted as the precipitating event of his first absence.

(b and c)  Two single male kitchen porters, one diagnosed as having had a nervous breakdown, involving seventeen years' hospitalization (clearly schizophrenic), the other, diagnosed schizophrenic with six years in hospital, may be treated together. Both taken on by the same firm, both living in a hostel, they did not appear from their records to be sufficiently well recovered to justify describing their readmissions as real relapses. Over-active, over-talkative, unable to concentrate, hiding in cupboards, absconding from the workplace, threatening their workmates and identifying authority with Nazism, both of them were clearly very unwell.

However, one had lasted a year, the other fifteen months. We know from the literature that patients who according to clinical criteria are indeed unwell are none the less capable of hanging on to jobs. But searching the records for triggering events, nothing specific stands out. Simply it looked as if the whole work scene provided more pressure than they could eventually tolerate.

(d)  A twenty-five year old copy typist in a teaching hospital engineer's office had a row with a ward sister, after which she left, and though she subsequently returned it was only a few weeks before she was admitted to psychiatric ward. The record reads: 'Relapse of schizophrenia: return of delusions, ill-understood by her fellow workers.'

Finally, from the group whose 'relapses' involved hospital read-mission, we present the records relating to two single women. It is not easy to attribute a precise triggering event either home or work based to their relapses, but they are of interest as illustrating the situation of a clearly identifiable section of the population at risk.

(a) A female clerical worker aged fifty-seven had joined the firm from school and had forty-one years' service. She lived at home by herself. Diagnosed as suffering from reactive depression with disturbance of thought, she was discharged in 1973 from her one previous admission, which had been of eight weeks' duration. In August, the first month of the record period, she was on holiday with two relatives and reported as 'very anxious in case she may cause trouble'. By October, her attitude to work had deteriorated and she was very anxious and depressed. By November the entry read: 'Deteriorated rapidly, work hopeless.' After three months' psychiatric sickness absence which included seven weeks in hospital, her work and behaviour records showed great improvement and the report was: 'Supervisor is pleased with improvement in condition.' Next month read: 'There is continual improvement in this patient who is working well and much happier.' For the remaining three months of the period her time-keeping was erratic but she had successfully absorbed slightly more responsibility. The medical officer's final comment: 'her main problem is lack of self-confidence. Does not like living alone', seems to offer the true explanation of the troubles experienced by an aging, lonely spinster.

(b) This case is similar to the one above. This employee, a single woman of fifty, a wiring and jigging operative of thirty years' service, also lived on her own. The record revealed nothing unusual until her work deteriorated necessitating in-patient admission for two months.

On her return to work she 'kept visiting surgery for treatment when there was nothing wrong with her, just wanted to roam around. Was in surgery at 7.30 one day but does not normally start till 8.' The researcher's amateur diagnosis is of chronic loneliness similar to the previous subject.

The second group absent more than ten working days might be re-garded as having less severe problems, as their relapses did not involve the necessity of hospital admission. The dichotomy of home- and work-based triggering events is also a useful one for this group. However the impression on the whole is of long-standing difficulties, frustrations, even misery, which suddenly the employee can no longer tolerate, rather than of critical, triggered, relapse episodes.

The first examples are those where home situations are mentioned. Two sickness absences at least appear as the direct result of marital problems. One man had instituted separation proceedings and was living in the same house as his wife but not with her. He then left the company and the district. Another, a senior research scientist, was living alone in the family home 'because of his wife's and daughter's mental state'. A third and fourth case were less clear-cut, in that both home and work events contribute. A clerical officer of fifty-one, diagnosed as suffering from an anxiety state, had marital problems but was also given to verbal outbursts out of frustration at his lack of promotion. A male nurse in his thirties, who suffered from agoraphobia after being dragged by a bus at the age of eight, was reported as having friction at home but also with his colleagues at work. Loneliness contributes again, where the subject's son had joined the Guards leaving him, a widower, on his own. All these cases appeared to be situations rather than episodes.

There are similarly cases where a work-based situation became intolerable. Five of these are given as illustrations.

(a) An employment manager whose job had been changed to a slower-paced one of career development officer a month before he went sick and left the company.

(b) A paranoid schizophrenic clerical officer of fifty-six years of age and eighteen years' service who suddenly realized he was not giving value for money, and had begun to talk of early retirement before he was sent home as unable to concentrate.

(c) A single female cashier-saleswoman of thirty-three, a schizo-phrenic living with her parents, worked three days a week and was first reported to be living in a world of her own, failing to concentrate. She was reduced from three to two working days, and because she could not choose which two days these should be, became upset and went sick. Later she was reported as 'much happier', having gained in confidence.

(d) A male technical illustrator of twenty-seven, schizophrenic, lived with his parents. In February 1976 he asked to see the firm's doctor, feeling himself that his symptoms were worse. There followed 'complaints of voices and eyes turning upwards', and six weeks' absence. On his return: 'Owing to complexity of work it seems to be a bit much of a strain and to pull him down.' He was advised to change his job for his own good, and went on half-time until he found a job at a swimming pool. The final comment: 'I feel it should be said that this chap was never of high standard as an illustrator and has always had to struggle to keep up' explains the difficulty, which was a long-standing one since he had been with the company for five years.

(e) Diagnosed manic-depressive, a married labourer of fifty-four with two years' hospitalization behind him lived in a semi-hostel type hospital ward. His record showed many unexplained absences, until finally came: 'Inability to cope with work situation. Would leave company transport en route to roam around town.'

This could however well be the description of an ill man who was never really up to working at all.

The events associated with the shorter sickness absences do not at first glance appear to differ in kind or severity from those associated with the longer absences. Two cases offered no clue, the employee being already absent at the start of the record. We judged the remaining four to consist of two work-based, and two home-based causes of absence. Of the two cases adjudged work-based, one, a West Indian woman out of hospital ten years, was recorded as moving to a more distant flat, and as working under a new buyer in the same month that she went psychiatrically sick. She also felt discriminated against racially ('probably with reason', wrote the record-keeper). On balance, it looks as if her work troubles were the greater. Also undoubtedly work-based was the reason behind the endogenous depressive who could not cope with shifts, and went sick when he should have been on nights.

Home-based, one surmises, was the anxiety of the man who went sick for a few days when his sixteen year-old daughter disappeared and was found a stowaway.

On such fragile information as that outlined above, attempts at quantification have limited value. For about half the fifty-three subjects, it was impossible to tell what, if anything, was associated with the relapse of absence; the remaining half were about equally divided between those experiencing home-based events or situations, and those experiencing work-based ones. Interestingly, we were told by a senior civil service medical adviser that the impression of his department also was of a 50:50 ratio between home and work-based triggers. The social worker at the Central Middlesex Occupational Health Service (Watson 1967), analysing the cases of 183 workers presenting with symptoms of severe emotional stress, found that sexual and matrimonial problems predominated. Only two instances of distress were connected with their employment. (This series was not confined to former patients, though twenty-eight were receiving or had received psychiatric treatment.)

How does all this tie in with Professors Wing and Brown's most recent research, in which the concept of a triggering life event has been supplemented by the minutely documented observations of 'E.E.', expressed emotion on the part of the relatives of relapsing patients?

Quite well. Professors Wing and Brown and their colleagues are dealing with discharged schizophrenics, the majority of whom will presumably go home, and mostly stay home. Our own small sample consisting of schizophrenics, depressives, and neurotics has a different life-style. Physically, they are away from home whilst at work. Emotionally, they will have invested varying degrees of their available emotional capital in their work; in the cases of the fifty year-old spinsters, a good proportion, it would appear. The emotion invested in their work makes them vulnerable in the same way as the schizo-phrenics at home are vulnerable to the expressions of disapproval voiced by their relatives in the Wing and Brown studies. At the same time they are not immune to home pressures, or home solitudes.

The above open-ended element of our data is not the sort to generate the precision of the Wing and Brown 'E.E.' results; but crude as it is, it may serve as a reminder that ex-patients at the top end of the clinical and employment scale will encounter pressures and emotional trauma sufficient to upset their precarious balance at the hands of others besides their relatives.

It is of interest to observe that no single case is reported of an inhuman assembly line causing relapse or absence. There are two cases of shift-work doing so.

### Relapse and diagnosis

For the overall population of former psychiatric hospital in-patients, relapse rates as measured by readmissions to hospital differ between diagnostic groups. However, the fact that the ex-patient has obtained employment seems to act as a levelling influence in this respect. *Table 8(3)* illustrates the finding that schizophrenics in our study are no more likely to relapse than are depressive or neurotics. Examination of the factors leading to relapses in each diagnostic group indicated that the patterns of relapse were also similar.

An employee with one diagnosis is just as likely as an employee with another diagnosis to experience sexual, marital, and boy or girl friend problems: divorces, separations, revulsions, expulsions, the seeking of asylum in hospital away from the marriage partner.

Table 8(3) *Proportions having some psychiatric sickness absence or hospital admission within diagnostic groups*

| diagnosis | % | size of diagnostic group |
|---|---|---|
| psychoses | 27 | 30 |
| reactive depression | 20 | 68 |
| all other depressions | 37 | 30 |
| neuroses | 28 | 32 |
| other diagnoses | 20 | 20 |
| all diagnoses | 29 | 180 |

The one exception becomes apparent when family worries are analysed. No schizophrenic is reported as relapsing for this reason. It is those diagnosed as depressed or neurotic who worry about their son leaving home to go to university, or to join the Guards, or to get married, or being made redundant. They worry about the daughter who stays out late, or disappears and stows away, or develops anorexia nervosa. Even the anniversary of a family death is mentioned in connection with one absence.

Pressure of work is reported as affecting individuals from all diagnostic categories. In the three cases where difficulties with shift-work are mentioned, two are depressive, one neurotic, none schizophrenic. The paranoid reaction of the worker whose record is outlined in (a) of page 134 is of interest. This man, diagnosed as depressive, and as coping successfully for a time with extra work pressure, absented himself at the point when four extra men were drafted to his section to help cope with it.

What does differ is the reported reaction of differently diagnosed ex-patients. The typical schizophrenic reaction is to be observed in three of the eight reports of schizophrenics relapsing: the hallucination of eyes turning upwards; the paranoid threatening of work-mates in a thoroughly disrupted work situation; the man who used to leave the company transport *en route* to the factory in order to wander aimlessly round town. Such extreme reactions were not reported among the other categories.

## Coping with a relapsed employee

'In case of sudden relapse, whom would you contact?' was the wording of one question in 1973. The answers to it are summarized below. At that date, Sample C medical officers turned most frequently to the family doctors (whom they might well know personally on the doctors' network), whereas Sample B employers and Remploy works managers turned most often to the hospitals. At that date, before the reorganization of local government, the social service departments figured infrequently in the replies: if the study were replicated today, it would almost certainly portray their far more active involvement.

Table 8(4)   *Agencies contacted by employers in event of relapse: survey 1973*

| employer | number of times mentioned in replies | | |
| | family doctor | local authority | hospital |
| --- | --- | --- | --- |
| Remploy | 20 | 16 | 34 |
| Sample B | 18 | 12 | 100 |
| Sample C | 119 | 27 | 75 |

We received evidence of the difficulty employers had in persuading anybody to deal with a relapsed patient. One Remploy works manager was so incensed that he telephoned us his experiences, which we noted as follows:

'The first occasion the difficulty arose was when a patient relapsed at 2 pm and it was 8 pm before he was admitted. Nobody could be contacted. The hospital denied responsibility. His own GP could not be contacted. If you got another GP there was the ethical problem between the two doctors. Meanwhile no-one, at the time of the reorganization of the Social Services Department, could be found there. Remploy staff were running round in all directions and the position was intolerable. Even if you got a social worker, he had to get clearance from a doctor, and if he could not, the only alternative is to get the employee admitted on an order, which nobody wants.

The Remploy manager therefore got hold of the Head of the Social Service Department, and said he could not take any more psychiatrically disabled workers, as he was meant to do, unless the Social Service Department could guarantee prompt action in the event of a relapse. So the Remploy factory now has a list of all the appropriate social workers' telephone numbers, and agreement has been reached between this worker's GP and the hospital doctor that he should be readmitted as necessary; and his GP will send a note afterwards.

This particular man in fact did suffer another relapse, and, under the new arrangements, was back in hospital 25 miles away in two hours.'

A firm of market gardeners wrote that their experience in employing ex-psychiatric patients had 'not been too good'.

'One of the reasons is that after a time, they are inclined to lapse back into their old ways and in two particular cases their trouble originated from alcohol and this is where the relapse occurred.

Our biggest problem was that when they came to us, they did well and naturally they applied for their discharge and when eventually they were granted this, and we noticed a deterioration in their condition, nobody wanted to know about it. On one occasion having tried all departments concerned to inform them about this we were told that they couldn't do anything about it until they did something wrong again and no doubt if the police picked them up they would be sent back for treatment.

Consequently, I have not been interested in employing any more'.

A point worthy of note is the extent to which hospitals are still referred to in emergency, despite the fact that mental illness is consciously being steered towards community treatment. One reason may be that hospitals have the advantage of always being there, whereas family doctors and social workers go off on their rounds. However efficient their base telephone-manning may be, delay is inevitable, which, at the very least, may be extremely inconvenient to an employer.

But the question must be asked: will the hospitals always be there, in the sense of having beds available for emergency use? The policy of emptying the hospitals and taking down beds makes this by no means a rhetorical question.

One possible solution has been suggested both by the telephoning Remploy manager and also by an occupational health doctor working for one of the biggest companies in the country:

A psychiatric hospital has a peculiar legal status. Under the 1959 Act a patient may of his own free will enter a psychiatric hospital as he would any other, but if he lacks the insight to be aware of his illness, a time-consuming procedure must be completed before he may be admitted. Our two respondents think a hospital should have authority to admit a patient in emergency without a committal order, and keep him in for twenty-four hours. The doctor quoted wrote to us evidently much distressed at what had happened to one of his firm's long-service employees, a schizophrenic who stopped his medication, had no insight, would not see his doctor, was not certifiable, and ultimately lost his job. Both suggest writing a clause into the Act.

A further point relates to psychiatric hospitals and their liaison with firms, particularly over medical certificates. Apparently some psychiatric hospitals simply omit to send these to employers, presumably for fear of divulging patients' whereabouts which they consider to be confidential information. To a factory welfare officer in Case Study B, this caused great inconvenience. It could happen that the firm's workers would be admitted to hospital and the firm would be none the wiser. No one would know where they were. The Welfare Department could send them a 'where are you?' letter and they could even be dismissed. General hospitals, it was said, contrive to send the firm a sick note, but the psychiatric hospital somehow sends the note straight off to Social Security without a copy coming to the factory.

An actual case illustrating absence of liaison with this co-operative factory sprang fresh to the welfare officer's mind. A shorthand-typist, a chronic patient, had worked well for seven months before relapsing. She was in fact still sleeping in hospital, but had returned to work two days previously without anyone in authority in the firm having the slightest idea that she was back.

This same firm has provided the most vivid example in our files of a family doctor, in close liaison with everyone concerned, dealing with a relapse at work. The case is that of a female electronics factory worker, diagnosed officially as suffering from 'nervous breakdown', though unofficially viewed as schizophrenic, on whom records were kept for a fourteen month period.

Daisy, who was born in 1917, had started full-time work in March 1969 while still sleeping at the local psychiatric hospital. In April 1971 she moved into a flat of her own. When the record period started in June 1972, she had been working for the past two and a half years on a VHF tuner picture test. Her foreman, who knew all her circumstances, found her a constant, reliable, good worker, a good time-keeper, who got on well with her colleagues. Her clothes were smart and she cared for her appearance.

As soon as the record started it was evident that she was actively hallucinating while still giving every satisfaction at her job. The record entries throughout the year report bizarre stories of her having been a film star, collecting money owing to her in America and so forth. Yet when promoted to inspector in a newly opened department the foreman could report that she was coping well with the extra responsibility.

However, in June 1973 the relapse occurred.

Wed. June 13    Daisy's foreman came to report some oddness about her. She is sure her console is not working well, but maintenance department have checked this and there are no problems. Daisy seems a little agitated but well.

Mon. June 18    Daisy came to surgery at 11 am with a reactive rash due to soap powder. Patient disorientated, talking about childhood and marriage in a Russian church to John Wayne. Appointment made to see our doctor.

Tues. June 19    Daisy back to work today, but very sleepy and tired. It seems her doctor wishes her to go to hospital for a 'check up' but since she is not 'a mental patient and her disorder is due to her blood' she would prefer not to.

After a telephone conversation with her doctor's secretary it was decided to try to keep her at work until Friday when transport could be arranged to take her to the psychiatric hospital's out-patient department.

Daisy's superintendent is worried but both he and her line foreman are being very co-operative as her output on the line is now very poor and she has to be constantly supervised.

Mon. June 25    Daisy is in work today, but very agitated and aggressive. She states that she is not going to accept treatment from hospital and is not going to stay at home either.

Her work output in the last two hours is nil and she is making 'rejects' so her supervisor feels he can carry her no longer. A further appointment is made with her GP after a talk on the telephone. He is going to undertake the treatment prescribed for her by the hospital and she will be on the sick register for the next two weeks.

Tues. July 10    Daisy returned to work today, much better, and almost back to her old self, her work output is a little slow. Her doctor had administered her injections twice weekly.

Fri. July 27        Works shut-down! Daisy is not going away for her three weeks' holiday, but says she's a little tired and will rest and catch up on her letter-writing.

Thus ends the faithful chronicle of a relapse, successfully managed by supervision, works' surgery, and family doctor with excellent liaison between all three.

Further examples illustrate varying degrees of employers' concern and other matters.

(a) A fifty-four year old divorced woman assembler, of whom it was suspected that depression aggravated her alcoholism was eventually admitted to hospital after reports that she was at loggerheads with other residents in her bedsitting room accommodation and that her concentration at work had deteriorated. She was notified by the firm that her employment would be suspended for one year unless she produced a medical certificate declaring her completely fit. She received this letter on her discharge from hospital on September 19 1976 and took an overdose on September 21. She was returned from the acute hospital to the psychiatric unit upon recovery. The record ceased at that point.

(b) A fitter's mate, suffering from depression, was placed on day work instead of shift-work while working from hospital, and still sleeping there. The following entry then appeared:– 'Manager and wife instructed by psychiatrist to threaten him with losing his job, and his wife to say she would leave him, in effort to shock him into pulling himself together again. It worked. He started to improve from then on.' Unfortunately it is plain that the improvement was short-lived. For the next four months the reports were of switching from shifts to days, and back again, but finally 'his fellow workers, at first most helpful, found it difficult to work with him on shifts because he was no unreliable. They had to go behind him tightening nuts that he should already have tightened. There was a risk of someone being seriously hurt'. When prolonged in-patient treatment again became necessary, his employment was terminated.

(c) This man's case had already been quoted as an example of marital difficulty leading to short sickness absence. Just at the point where the twelve-month record ceased, a note was appended stating that this schizophrenic engineering craftsman had resigned of his own volition having himself decided that he needed full-time hospital treatment. 'He resigned from the company against the firm advice of the Personnel Department but was promised his job back if he so wished on his discharge from hospital.'

Considering such evidence, the question may again be posed: 'To whom should firms have recourse in the event of relapse?' The welfare officer of Case Study Firm B was clear in her own mind that it should depend upon whom it was that the ex-patient had had a therapeutic relationship with in the past. If the employee had discussed his troubles with a social worker, she would contact him; if with a psychiatric hospital nurse, she would contact him. Judging by the evidence presented in *Table 8(4)*, it looks as if it is the employer's therapeutic relationship, not the patient's, which at present determines to whom he will have recourse.

## After a relapse

A perusal of our records and correspondence files with medical officers, Remploy works managers, and employers' various representatives illustrates the imaginative care and concern often bestowed upon the long-service employee who has suffered psychiatric breakdown. This is an aspect of the matter very little publicized, in our view.

The opportunity arose for a quite lengthy discussion of several practical devices aimed at smoothing the return to work of a psychiatrically, or for that matter, physically disabled employee. This was with the Group Medical Officer in charge of the occupational health of the 12,000 employees comprising Case Study Firm C. Quite possibly these practices are duplicated in other firms: we do not know, but hope so.

For example, if an employee of Firm C has been off sick for a considerable time, the Group Medical Officer has managed to persuade the local GPs to send him up to the works medical department a fortnight before he is due to be signed off on his final note. This arrangement is highly beneficial. It takes the emotion out of the situation which otherwise occurs when a man returns without warning on a Monday morning and sits there four-square in the personnel department demanding 'Where's my job?' It gives the personnel department time to make proper arrangements. They know they need not find work for the returned employee that instant, or else send him home and pay him – a depressing experience for someone all keyed up to return to work in any case. On occasion they have even got a GP to extend the sick leave period.

Another device gets round difficulties inherent in a labour cost budget: we know of at least one other company operating a similar system. At this plant the Group Medical Officer can arrange for a man to be carried for three or four weeks excess to budget: in the other firm he is a charge on a special extra-departmental rehabilitation Budget. The result is the same, giving a neutral period in which to run an employee back into harness again after his long lay-off. On such an occasion the doctor always arranges to see the man within the first four weeks after his return to work, and thereafter if individual circumstances require. This support assures the man that he is not being cast to the wolves, so to speak, without anyone routinely caring.

This Group Medical Officer and the Staff Medical Adviser of a large Department Store are two outstanding believers in supporting the foreman and supervisors also. 'Thank you for ringing me up and telling me about Mr X', for example. And 'Well done, Mr Y, in succeeding in keeping poor Miss Y on the rails for so long. I know it hasn't been easy.'

If he is advocating any unusual action the GMO takes care to send a memo to the personnel department and to the foreman concerned. This gives a foreman backing in case any slight bending of the rules should go wrong and land him in trouble with his supervisor. By the same token a doctor's note from outside the factory carries no executive weight within the factory, unless it goes through the medical department. The GMO insists on his ultimate responsibility in all health matters within the factory and these points logically follow.

This same doctor was probably the arch exponent of therapeutic counselling encountered during the six years. In the parent plant of 7,000 employees, he saw a total of thirty-nine with psychiatric symptoms of varying severeity in the course of thirteen months, the majority having probably two or three interviews. We calculated that this amounted to some eight interviews per month or two per week on these psychiatric cases alone, a proportion which illustrates the high priority attached by this doctor to this aspect of his work. Examples of these therapeutic review sessions were given. One such was a chief buyer, who had progressed to this senior post since his illness, an uncommon progression. This man had suffered from acute depression necessitating in-patient treatment at the time he was due for promotion. He took a lesser job, recovered, improved and then obtained a different chief buyer's job which he was successfully holding down. On his return from hospital, still in the acute stage, the GMO would see him as often as three days a week: then one day, then every few weeks, gradually tailing off. Often this would be at the end of the day, so that the patient would not lose time. Then they would perhaps drive home together.

A second man he spent a great deal of time on. This man's work often took him to Scandinavia. He was forever on and off aeroplanes. But he became over-pressured and the firm had to ground him while he received out-patient treatment. Gradually he did a few local flips to get his nerve back and from there, with the help of much sympathetic listening, he was able to return to his job.

Sympathetic listening: the ingredients for successful counselling would appear to be quite simply the capacity to listen, together with the relevant industrial, and psychiatric, know-how.

## Relapse and socio-economic drift

Besides presenting employers with an organizational problem, and employees with at the least a spell off work, relapse at work carries the potential of socio-economic drift. Sociologists' observations of the various forms of social deviance, including criminality and mental illness, have identified a drift phenomenon through the operation of which the mentally ill, amongst others, end up as over-represented in the lower occupational classes (Weinberg 1968). This has been investigated particularly extensively with regard to schizophrenia (Goldberg and Morrison 1963; Dunham 1964).

There has been less consensus as to how the phenomenon should be interpreted, but it would appear, in the case of schizophrenia, that the families of schizophrenics have the same socio-economic pattern as the population in general, but that the schizophrenics themselves, being handicapped by their illness from educational and occupational achievement, gravitate towards, or remain in, the lower occupational classes. The Psychiatric Rehabilitation Association, a voluntary organization concerned with both research and action in the East End of London, has documented the over-representation of the mentally ill in its own populations (Psychiatric Rehabilitation Association 1968 and 1969) and from it, has argued for a differential allocation of resources to these and similarly placed inner city areas.

So far, the hypothesis of downward drift in mental illness has been built on observations which do not extend to the employment field. This state of affairs may be remedied to some extent by consideration of the evidence gathered in the course of the research, which may well help to fill a gap in knowledge of the whole process.

The data came from the 1973 survey. They were provided by two sets of respondents and relate to two samples of established employees, who some time previously had received psychiatric hospital in-patient treatment but who were back at work by February 1973, the survey date.

Sample B is described in detail on page 59. It consisted of 130 co-operative employers in touch with the hospitals. The primary units of Sample C were firms employing industrial medical officers who were members of the Society of Occupational Medicine. They are described on page 61.

The 'old' employees are the ones whose records yielded information about relapses, since it was possible to ask 'before/after' questions about them.

The data collected were quantified in financial terms and in terms of occupational and social status: occupational status proved the most rewarding. *Table 8(5)* sets out the occupational status groups used in terms of the Registrar General's Socio-Economic Groups (1970). We also drew an additional distinction between machine operators and non-machine operators, since in some quarters ex-patients have been considered unsuitable for machine work and we wanted to look at the two groups separately.

Table 8(5)   *Occupations in terms of Registrar General's Socio-Economic Groups, 1970*

| | | | |
|---|---|---|---|
| I | SEGs | 1–4 | managers in large and small establishments; professional workers |
| II | SEGs | 5. 1 | ancillary workers and artists (nurses, teachers, laboratory assistants etc.) |
| | | 5. 2 | foremen and supervisors, non-manual |
| | | 8 | foremen and supervisors, manual |
| III | SEG | 6 | junior non-manual (clerks, typists, shop assistants, draughtsmen) |
| IV | SEG | 7 | personal service workers (cooks, canteen assistants, domestic staff) |
| V | SEG | 9 | skilled manual operating machines |
| VI | SEG | 9 | skilled manual *not* operating machines (upholsters) |
| VII | SEG | 10 | semi-skilled manual operating machines (m/c tool workers, presses) |
| VIII | SEG | 10 | semi-skilled manual *not* operating machines (assembly, inspection) |
| IX | SEG | 11 | unskilled (porters, messengers, labourers) |
| X | | | occupation not known |

*Source*: Wansbrough and Cooper 1978

What was the result? Who moved up? Who moved down, as a result of their relapse?

*Table 8(6)* gives the before/after picture in terms of occupation for the B sample of fifty-four old employees returning to work after relapse. It gives the picture as a whole, but masks the movements of individuals within the total. A count of these movements revealed that forty-four employees (81 per cent) went back to the same occupation as before, while nine moved down*, and one's original status was unknown. Thus five out of six employees remained in the same job and one out of six moved down.

Table 8(6) *The before/after situation in terms of occupation, Sample B provided by ninety-one employers liaising with the psychiatric hospitals in resettlement*

| class | number be- fore hospi- talization | occupation | number after hospi- talization |
|-------|------------------------------------|------------|--------------------------------|
| I | 4 | managers and professional workers | 4 |
| II | 4 | intermediate occupations | 1 |
| III | 9 | junior non-manual | 10 |
| IV | 3 | personal services | 3 |
| V | 2 | skilled machine operators | 1 |
| VI | 2 | skilled manual non-machine operators | 1 |
| VII | 5 | semi-skilled machine operators | 6 |
| VIII | 19 | semi-skilled *non* machine operators | 19 |
| IX | 5 | unskilled | 9 |
| X | 1 | occupation not known | 10 |
|  | 54 |  | 54 |

*Source*: Wansbrough and Cooper 1978

With regard to earnings, thirty-eight out of the fifty-four received the same amount as before hospitalization, four received more (which could have been national wage rises), four received less, and for eight the information was not available. As to another indicator, the capacity to undertake 'paced' work, this affected very few people. Five were thus employed before relapse of whom two moved off it. But on the other

---

* The nine who moved down were: Three from intermediate occupations to junior non-manual, semi-skilled machine operator and semi-skilled non-machine operator. One from junior non-manual to semi-skilled non-machine operator. One from skilled machine operator to semi-skilled machine operator. Four skilled and semi-skilled workers (one of whom had been a semi-skilled machine operator), down to unskilled work.

hand two employees not previously engaged on paced work, after hospitalization went on to it.

*Table 8(7)* sets out the before/after occupation picture for the 405 old employees of Sample C returning to their employment in open conditions after hospitalization. Investigating the effects on the individuals comprizing these totals, the count showed that 331 (82 per cent) of the 405 employees remained in the same jobs, and seventy-four (18 per cent) changed jobs. Of the seventy-four who changed jobs, forty-eight (12 per cent) went 'down' the table; one had an unknown occupation before entering hospital; thirteen went 'up'; and eleven went to unknown occupations after hospital. Here indeed was the downward occupational drift – 12 per cent – which people have come to expect. Probably more surprising was the upward movement of thirteen (3 per cent) members of this sample, though for seven of them the move was from a manual to a clerical job.

Within each occupational category some interesting results emerged. For instance, three of the five Managers (Class 1) went down to Junior Non-Manual (Class III) but one came up from that class. In fact altogether seven moved out of the Junior Non-Manual or clerical class to various other classes, while twelve people from other classes moved into it. These twelve who were in effect fixed up with a clerical job, comprised the three Managers, two Class II 'Intermediate' and seven skilled and semi-skilled manual workers. However, the most striking

Table 8(7)    *The before/after situation in terms of occupation: Sample C provided by ninety-nine industrial medical officers*

| class | number be-<br>fore hospi-<br>talization | occupation | number<br>after hospi-<br>talisation |
|---|---|---|---|
| I | 46 | managers and professional workers | 42 |
| II | 44 | intermediate occupations | 39 |
| III | 58 | junior non-manual | 63 |
| IV | 5 | personal services | 4 |
| V | 28 | skilled machine operators | 19 |
| VI | 45 | skilled manual non-machine operators | 33 |
| VII | 36 | semi-skilled machine operators | 25 |
| VIII | 96 | semi-skilled non-machine operators | 105 |
| IX | 46 | unskilled | 64 |
| X | 1 | occupation not known | 11 |
| | 405 | | 405 |

*Source*: Wansbrough and Cooper 1978

effects were to be observed amongst the skilled workers (Classes V and VI). No less than twenty-five, (36 per cent) underwent a change of job on returning to work, the majority of sixteen went down to semi-skilled or unskilled occupations, five to clerical work, and four to unknown occupations.

It is these figures which lead to the questioning of the thesis, put forward by Dr Douglas Bennett amongst others, that for mentally ill people it is 'role' performance rather than 'task' performance which causes difficulty. The results of all the moves just described are to be seen in the expanded totals of the semi-skilled non-machine workers of Class VIII and the unskilled workers of Class IX.

To complete the picture it should be reported that 234 (58 per cent) of the 405 continued to earn the same as they had before, for 111 the information was not available, and thus the recorded changes in earnings, up or down, affected only about sixty (15 per cent) of the sample.

Summarizing, five out of six employees in Sample B and four out of five in Sample C, admitted for hospital in-patient treatment, returned to their old jobs after one particular episode of illness.

This is the broad scene. Having established it, we felt we wanted to know if there were any important characteristics distinguishing those who had stayed put from those who had had to move down. We therefore examined the retrospective records of each employee's behaviour and performance at work, in which were noted any complaints of odd, disagreeable, or dangerous behaviour; excessive sickness absence or slow work. In Sample B, there was no indication that those who had moved down behaved any differently from those whose occupation had remained unchanged. However, there was evidence that they had attracted more complaints of excessive sickness absence and slow work. None of this showed up in Sample C.

Sample C, however, provided through its medical officers information on diagnosis. This is summarized in relation to the direction of job change in *Table 8(8)* figures which indicate that the direction of movement of people suffering from depression is up the socio-economic scale and significantly different from the movement of the other diagnostic groups.

For both Sample B and Sample C there was no difference in the pattern of job changes in different age groups, nor for Sample C in the patterns of different durations of employment.

The last things to look at in this connection are the reasons for termination of employment, for some employees experienced relapses of a severity which prevented their returning to work at all. The question

Table 8(8)   *Primary diagnosis and a change of job*
*after hospitalization for Sample C*

| | job change | | |
|---|---|---|---|
| *primary diagnosis* | up | *no change* | *down* |
| psychoses | I | 60 | 12 |
| depressions | 10 | 193 | 20 |
| neuroses | I | 41 | 11 |
| others | I | 31 | 4 |

Table 8(9)   *Reasons for leaving: numbers leaving and (percentages) of all those leaving within samples*

| | Sample B (employers liaising with hospitals) | | Sample C (industrial Medical Officers) | |
|---|---|---|---|---|
| *reason* | *(i) 54 old employees* | *(ii) 242 new employees* | *(i) 405 old employees* | *(ii) 148 new employees* |
| re-admission to hospital | 1 (11) | 21 (23) | 1 (2) | 0 (0) |
| mental illness | 0 (0) | 6 (6) | 0 (0) | 2 (8) |
| Physical illness, pregnancy, or unspecified illness | 1 (11) | 4 (4) | 5 (9) | 1 (4) |
| redundant, unsuitable or discharged | 3 (33) | 22 (24) | 19 (36) | 4 (16) |
| failed to report | 0 (0) | 15 (16) | 1 (2) | 2 (8) |
| other (including moving from area, another job, retired, died) | 2 (22) | 21 (23) | 16 (30) | 6 (23) |
| reason not known | 2 (22) | 4 (4) | 11 (21) | 11 (42) |
| all reasons | 9 | 93 | 53 | 26 |
| ° leaving (all reasons) | 16.7 | 38.4 | 13.1 | 17.6 |

*Source*: Wansbrough and Cooper 1978

was: how many? *Table 8(9)* tells the story. It shows that for the old employees of both samples, and also for the new employees of Sample C, 'readmission to hospital' was a minor reason for leaving. Not so for the newly engaged employees of the compassionate B employers: for them 'readmission to hospital' figured prominently. These in fact were the 'trial balloons', the people mostly taken on straight from hospital, whose capacity for living and working in the community had demonstrably been only precariously established.

All in all, this particular analysis has, we believe, led to a useful infilling of the 'drift' hypothesis, and has led also to some definition of an ex-in-patient's working expectations. This is provided its limitations are borne in mind. The first of these of course is the non-random character of the two respondent samples – so often emphasized. There is no doubt that we are operating at the compassionate end of the labour market, and that this is practically bound to lead to unusually benevolent personnel practices in this sort of area. Second, the data relate to a single episode of hospital admission for each individual. And third, the figures cannot specify how often individuals re-enter hospital and whether episodes represent first or subsequent admissions.

If the latter, there is no doubt that repeated too often, readmissions will try the patience of any employer beyond endurance, and the ex-patient's employment will be terminated (Martin and Morgan 1975).

# 9

## The attitudes and experiences
## of employers

The resistance put up by most employers against hiring anyone with a history of mental illness is deep seated and well known. It was spelled out by John Martin, who in his study *Offenders as Employees* listed eighteen reasons given by employers for turning down men applying for jobs. A history of mental illness came third in the list, after 'straightforward lack of ability' and 'physical health' and ahead of the knowledge that the applicant had a criminal record. But some employers do accept these applicants, and to find out why they do, and why some do it more successfully than others, were among the reasons for undertaking the research programme.

The differing standpoints of the three groups of respondents need to be borne in mind when considering what they have to say. The Remploy works managers, for example, have to accept the mentally and physically disabled because the provision of work for them is their *raison d'être*. The Sample B employers are, to the greatest extent in the study, free to exercise their own discretion as to whether or not they hire an ex-patient: they really are 'employers'. The medical officers in Sample C, on the other hand, usually operate in a capacity which is technically advisory to the personnel or line managers who make the ultimate employment decisions – unless the offer of a job is made specifically dependent on the result of a medical examination.

### Willingness to go on employing ex-patients

It might be supposed that the clearest indication of a management's attitude towards employing ex-patients would lie in their preparedness to go on doing so. If their experience is too unhappy they will not; and indeed, the importance of selecting 'good' ex-patients for a job with a new employer has been stressed to us in contacts with referring hospitals, for the sake of those who may follow. Similarly one is reminded of the practice of the nursing officer in the northern city, who the minute one patient broke down in a good, suitable job, promptly supplied the employer with another to keep it warm (Interim Report November 1971). Respondents were therefore asked by questionnaire, 'Are you prepared to go on employing ex-psychiatric hospital patients?', with the result shown in *Table 9(1)*.

Table 9(1)   *Are you prepared to go on employing ex-patients?*

| sample | yes | no | no answer | total |
|--------|-----|-----|-----------|-------|
| Pilot | 10 | 0 | 3 | 13 |
| Remploy | | not applicable | | |
| B | 109 | 15 | 7 | 131 |
| C | 140 | 2 | 6 | 148 |

In addition, the industrial medical officers of Sample C were asked whether they would re-employ their own employees who had entered a psychiatric hospital for in-patient treatment, with an even higher preponderance of affirmative answers (195 'sometimes'; twelve 'almost always'; one 'very rarely'; two 'never'). All these replies suggest that respondents feel that they ought, in suitable conditions, to employ ex-patients, particularly if they did so before they became ill. And yet there is the contrary evidence, quantified below and widely acknowledged elsewhere, how few in fact, when it comes to the point, will do so.

As a start, the actual composition of our samples is significant. Asked to provide data (to a maximum of six per category) on two categories of ex-patients, their own employees who had broken down on the one hand, and newcomers to the firm on the other, ninety-two participating doctors in Sample C were able to list old employees to the number of 407, but only 145 new ones between them. Again, in the D sample, only 16 per cent of the 180 ex-patients studied had been recognised as such at the time they were taken on; for 80 per cent the discovery was made subsequently, indicating that employers had not hired them knowingly.

Thus employers' actions did not bear out expressed good intentions. There may be a methodological explanation for this. Among attitude surveys, political polls frequently prove inaccurate as predictors of actual voting as distinct from expressed voting intentions. Similar doubts persist about answers to a simple forced-choice question as a valid predictor of employing action (as distinct from employing intention). Respondents may well have replied as they thought they ought to reply.

Despite this qualification, it is legitimate to use the answers received in an attempt to discover what factors are associated with an employer's stated willingness to go on employing ex-patients. For example, it is a question of evident importance to what extent an employer is influenced by the support offered to him by family practitioner, local authority, and hospital services. For the Sample B employers (those pre-eminently decision-taking) it was clear that a higher proportion of those dissatisfied with their supporting service were indeed not prepared to go on employing ex-patients ($p = 0.12$) though the numbers were small.

Further correlations were tested, and there was a hint that firms endowed with doctors, nurses, personnel officers, and uncles persisted with ex-patients more often than firms without these officers. This was the type of result one might expect. Also to be expected with the trend for those organizations which had a specific policy, and those which reminded patients to take their tablets, to be more prepared than the others to continue taking ex-patients. In analyses by type of organization, there was very little to choose between industry, public services, distributive services and the matrons of old people's homes: attitudes and experiences did not divide along these lines.

The other main source of information upon which to build an estimate of attitudes was the respondents' open-ended comments, all of which were systematically analysed.

### Remploy works managers

Remploy experience was very mixed. Forty-three works managers responded to the invitation to open ended comment, and of these fifteen made replies reflecting generally favourable experience, eleven generally unfavourable, while the other seventeen could not be classified as predominantly favourable or unfavourable.

The importance of correct placing in a suitable job, and of disposing of an adequate variety of jobs from which to choose was mentioned by six works managers. Nine mentioned the need for closer supervision than that required by other categories of disabled workers – these were points which naturally impressed themselves on the minds of shop-floor managers. Otherwise, their comments broadly coincided with those of the medical officers; and referred to poor and unreliable attendance, unpredictable behaviour which could upset other workers, and lack of discipline with regard to medication. One wrote specifically of the difficulties of the first weeks in employment, thus: 'The employees who work the three months' trial period usually stay on. The crisis period is usually the first week, some progress well but then crack up: others back out.' Thus experience in Remploy is varied. Yet even in respect of workers recognized as so disabled as to qualify for sheltered work provision, a third of the managers replying judged their experience as having been mainly successful.

### Sample B

Eighty-one respondents of the 131 compassionate employers comprising Sample B availed themselves of the invitation to open-ended comment.

First, an attempt was made by means of a straightforward count to assess how many had mainly satisfactory experiences and how many the reverse. This was an almost impossible task because so many employers reported experience both good and bad. It appeared that some thirty-four had chiefly good experience and eighteen outright bad experience, with a shaded area in between consisting of mixed experiences and qualified statements.

### Industry

By far the great majority of jobs were to be found in industry. Three employers were unreservedly enthusiastic.
One wrote:

'I have only engaged one person, who I know to be a psychiatric case, and she was a resident of X hospital, but came to work for us for approximately 3 years. She worked with 2 other women on the packing-despatch bench. She obviously "lived on her nerves", but was an able worker, very keen, never late, and I was sorry when she left. I engaged her against other people's advice, initially for a trial period of 3 months. She stayed 3 years and never let me down.'

Another:

'I personally was responsible for starting this system and get great pleasure from seeing ex-patients blossom into real people again. Even more rewarding is the tremendous amount of good seen to be done to other workers by letting them become involved and interested in the well being of people who have been less fortunate than themselves.'

And the third:

'With the co-operation of hospital doctors and ward sisters and their awareness of our limitations and requirements we are able to eliminate the basic problems. We in turn have had close contact with the hospital and recognise our responsibilities in selecting employment suitable for the type of exercise. From an employer's angle, having had over 3 years some 25 to 30 patients through these works, it has been a pleasure to have people who want to work and appreciate working with a will.'

Others reported cautious if limited satisfaction, ex-patients being described as 'normally quite good', 'reasonably good, getting on with fellow-workers', 'always found to be of value to us', and so on. The qualifications expressed were those of the Remploy managers: the need for careful selection and placement, and for good supervision on the employers' side; and on the ex-patients' side, possible slowness, dislike of change, preference for routine, and propensity to worry. A number observed completely contrasting patterns of behaviour among the ex-patients they had known. One had found his employees 'either hardworking and conscientious or no use at all, there doesn't seem to be any in between; in fact most seem over-anxious to please'. Another found that 'those who do adapt are generally very loyal and willing'. From the employers' angle perhaps the most infuriating characteristic is that of the patients who turn up only promptly to disappear – particularly when any kind of training is involved: 'the three we have had worked alright, but after a few weeks all three just walked out and did not return'.

Not all depart so hastily: 'eight men have been with us since 1959 and 1960: one since 1967: two since 1970: a record which appears to confirm the view that patients tend either *to* settle well, or not *to* settle at all.

### Residential, hospital and local authority work

This sample of employers included a proportion of employers in residential, hospital, and local authority work such as has for long been thought particularly suitable for the ex-psychiatric patient because of the support available. Experiences here were as mixed as anywhere, and by no means altogether successful.

Among the satisfied employers was the matron of a small home caring for eight old ladies. She had employed successively four patients still living in the local hospital, three of them most satisfactory and the fourth still with her, a very happy part of the household, doing odd jobs and shopping for the residents as well as her domestic work and with two years' service to her credit. The matron of a larger old people's home had employed one woman for eight years who had always worked extremely well under direction – still living in hospital and still on medication. Other hospitals and nursing homes, and a small school, reported on reasonable standards of work, and the need for good supervision. Some had been satisfactory both as regards behaviour and work pattern, others not. One of the most satisfactory cases reported upon was that of a domestic worker who had been subsequently promoted to Assistant Matron, a job she proved well capable of holding down.

The following letter from a hotel manageress is illustrative of the attitude of a sympathetic employer who has been given little to go on:

'From my own experience, the employment of ex-psychiatric patients has been satisfactory. I have employed three persons during the past 7 years, and although one case could have been deemed a "failure", she made a good recovery after further hospital treatment and is now holding down a responsible position. Unfortunately I was away when the relapse occurred and I feel very strongly that had I been available at the time it might never have happened.

At the present, I have a chambermaid who was a patient in hospital for over 20 years. This is her first post since leaving the hospital. She has been with me for just over 2 years. She has worked very satisfactorily on the whole and about 2 months ago I had my first unpleasant clash with her. She was very difficult and I am afraid my patience was exhausted, and I did in fact give her a week's notice – in my own defence, I was justified in doing so. However, she shed some tears and then later apologised to me and asked me to re-engage her. This I was pleased to do. She is about 52 years of age and going through her menopause which may account for her sudden change of attitude. Likewise her family now adult, who did not bother about her when she was in hospital, are now very prominent in her life and cause her quite a lot of concern with broken marriages, etc.

I have found with my chambermaid that she appreciates seeing the Welfare Officer and feels free to discuss her job with her – in other words the Welfare Officer takes the role of liaison officer between the employer and employee and can often pour oil on troubled waters. Unfortunately, probably due to pressure of work, the visits from the welfare authorities usually peter out after about 3 months from the patient leaving hospital.

Likewise for lay persons like myself a brief case history of the patient would be invaluable and also what attitude to adopt with them when difficulties arise.'

It is perhaps surprising that hospital employers should so often have reported less happy experience. Perhaps such employers, in view of the prevailing idea that they offer such suitable niches, are asked to take on less recovered patients. Thus to one hospital domestic superintendent they simply 'cause too many problems'. A domestic manager found that 'special care is needed in placing such staff in view of the possible effect on sick hospital patients'. This results in far more supervision and checking being necessary and in some cases, at times great worry for the supervisor in the area, when ex-psychiatric employees are observed to be in a 'bad cycle'. Another group domestic administrator had an extra difficulty to contend with:

> 'I find that it takes a great deal of real concern, and painstaking care, particularly on the part of supervisory staff, to make a success of such attempts at rehabilitation, for this is what they are. By far the greater majority of my women are prepared to make every possible allowance for those they regard as less fortunate than themselves, and the subjects receive maximum help from members of my domestic staff. Unfortunately, the same cannot be said always of the attitude of nursing staff towards ex-patients. This seems illogical, but is none the less true.'

Particular note was made of the comment proffered by four local authority officers. As with residential work, the idea has grown up that the job of council roadsweeper or park attendant is a suitable one. Two respondents pointed out that this is no longer so since the introduction of incentive bonus schemes.

One wrote:

> 'Experience not too good. Out of some 30 ex-psychiatric patients employed over the last 8 years or so only two have proved satisfactory for the type of work carried out by a local authority technical department. The recent introduction of incentive bonus schemes has made it even more difficult to place these patients.'

But incentive bonus schemes were not the only difficulty, for neither of the two other local authority officers reported satisfactory experience.

### Sample C occupational health doctors

A quick count of Sample C replies, showing respectively broadly favourable or broadly unfavourable experience and attitudes, revealed a dead-heat: twenty favourable and twenty unfavourable out of a total of some 180 comments. Most doctors, however, replied in terms not susceptible to this type of count. The prevailing attitude, following a reading of all the correspondence, could perhaps best be summed up in the neat phraseology of one respondent as 'benevolent pragmatism'. To which it must be added that some emphasize the benevolence and some the pragmatism.

Among the former, the defence departments, the nationalized industries, and at least two major local authorities appear to have formulated employment policies embodying concepts of social justice, to the effect that no applicant for work should be rejected on medical grounds unless these make him or her a source of danger to himself or others. Some doctors employed in the private sector expressed themselves as perhaps more keenly aware of the competitive winds that blow. Thus: 'The medically desirable has to be equated with the economically practical in competitive industry; a production department has to produce and meet targets.' And, 'Whilst we are always sympathetic to the needs of all ex-patients, I think the psychiatric hospital staff must also realize that we are a productive unit and must make a profit to survive, and we are not an extension of the medical services, not a convalescent centre.'

Nobody pretended that the employment of ex-psychiatric hospital patients is likely to be entirely problem-free, but one doctor at least made the point that only an extremely small minority cause problems through odd behaviour or acute breakdown: quantification of these occurrences is to be found in Chapters 6 and 8.

On the other hand, it was said that ex-patients require more supervision by medical departments than any other employees and that they involve welfare departments in time-absorbing supportive assistance to ex-patients and their families. It may fairly be observed, however, that that is what these departments are there for. More important is the impact on production departments. What difficulties, if any, are encountered on the shop floor or its equivalent? Again summarizing from an abundance of correspondence, these would appear to be five in number:

(1) A tendency towards excessive sickness absences.
(2) Relapses at work.
(3) Disturbance of the work of others.
(4) Difficulties of interpersonal relationships.
(5) Slow rehabilitation.

(1) The tendency towards excessive sickness absence was perhaps the commonest objection raised. As a result of it, the subject was investigated intensively in the Sample D study, on which quantitative data are assembled in Chapter 7. One doctor mentioned that the repeated and lengthy absences can be comparable to those encountered

in chronic physical disease such as rheumatoid arthritis or bronchitis.

From the point of view of the employee, whether he is able to be away on sick pay, or whether his employment is fairly abruptly terminated will depend largely on the type of sick pay scheme in force. One major local authority may well provide up to a year's sick pay entitlement in a case of psychiatric (or any other) illness.

(2) Relapses at work. The possibility of relapse, always present, continues to cause anxiety, not only on account of distress to the patient and disturbance to the work place, but on account of difficulties experienced in re-admitting an acute case to hospital – all matters dealt with in Chapter 8.

(3) Disturbance of others' work is mentioned by a medical officer in one of the nationalized industries as being the commonest complaint by management. 'Patients must not be allowed to indulge in departmental therapy, i.e. to be always talking about their problems to such an extent that no work is done by two people', writes another.

(4) Difficulties of interpersonal relationships. The senior medical officer of an occupational health service catering for 16,000 local authority employees of a variety of grades and working in twenty-five different departments, has already been quoted. He found that clerical or administrative posts, where teamwork and interpersonal relationships are essential, were not successful, and at best were tolerated only; but that manual occupations, particularly if the employee were working on his own, at his own pace, with sympathetic supervision, were most likely to succeed provided that sickness absences were not excessive. A doctor in private industry, whose experience had been mainly satisfactory, also reported his main trouble as being with people who have difficulty with interpersonal relationships. In fact a number of employers pointed to this difficulty. Together they suggested a line of thought which was pursued in the subsequent study of the D records. This was that the probable relative failure tentatively discerned in administrative and clerical posts may be due not to incapacity but to the necessity of working in small groups where interpersonal relationships are important. It was found (page 85) that small groups in offices were indeed trying, and more so than small groups elsewhere. No doubt the factor of stress, whereby steps up the administrative ladder bring greater responsibility for decision making and problem solving, is also involved, but this factor is now fairly generally recognized.

(5) On the subject of rehabilitation and the return to work, two points stand out among the comments received. The first is that a period of poor performance is to be expected. This is not surprising. The length of

the rehabilitation period necessary in psychiatric illness has been consistently underestimated, not least by the government departments involved. But the point to make, and one which is made by numbers of doctors, is that once the initial period has been surmounted, ex-patients can settle down to become the reliable employees of ten, twenty, and thirty years' service such as are to be found in our files.

At this point it is necessary to introduce a note of caution to employers who may find it difficult to decide whether this period of poor performance is, indeed, part of a process of long-term rehabilitation, or whether it is the result of inadequate recovery caused by premature discharge from hospital. Analysis of the D study (in which it will be recalled, the performance of 180 ex-patients is monitored over a twelve month period) indicates that 'Time since last discharge' correlates significantly with the onset of relapses: that is to say, it is found that those ex-patients who relapse are liable to be the ones most recently out of hospital. And how is an employer meant to distinguish who is on the point of further relapse and who is undergoing slow rehabilitation?

In either event, it is worth drawing attention to the practice of certain firms when rehabilitating their employees after a long lay-off. One such firm is Case Study C, where the medical officer is empowered to arrange that the wages of a worker returning after prolonged absence are a charge not on his department's budget, but on a special extra-departmental fund. This lasts for a specified period, and as may be readily imagined, makes the returning, less efficient worker much more popular with management and supervision than he would otherwise have been.

The same medical officer has arranged another way of easing such a worker's return. He has contacted all the general practitioners in the neighbourhood with the suggestion that they give him warning, a fortnight ahead, of sick or injured workers' impending re-entry. This gives time for matters to be sorted out.

The second point emphasized among the comments is that a firm's own employees following hospital treatment are invariably re-employed if possible in their original departments with their original colleagues. If this is found to be most successful, a common sense suggests that it will be, it highlights the stress to which a new employee will be subject when he takes up employment in an entirely new environment. Thus a doctor writing from a factory which is a closely knit community, where all the workforce tend to be related and the foremen visit their staff when sick, finds that his known patients never posed a problem. 'But the borderline schizoid, particularly if a new-comer to the factory and the area, with a history of treatment elsewhere, can be a problem. I am thinking here of young graduates with a university history of a breakdown.'

Two further matters of limited application but considerable interest, were brought up by single respondents. The first occurs in defence departments (and possibly elsewhere) where downgrading from a skilled to a labouring job not only has an adverse effect on current pay, but on gratuities and pensions which are based on the last year's pay. The second was raised by a medical officer in charge of a local authority occupational health service, who was concerned that so many applicants for teaching and social work posts exhibit a history of psychiatric illness, and considered that the authority might have a third party responsibility for young children in this connection.

## Co-operation and confidentiality

Co-operation among all concerned with the welfare of a patient is accepted as of prime importance, but in the present context of a patient's transition from the sick to the breadwinning role, the experience reported by occupational health doctors with their opposite numbers in the health service is very uneven.

Some firms evidently enjoy excellent relations with their neighbouring hospitals and units and can count on receiving full reports.

Several have codified their relations into questionnaire form. At one well-known company, all new employees coming from a mental hospital are asked to sign a form giving the industrial medical officer permission to approach his consultant psychiatrist. The latter is then sent this simple, direct questionnaire, asking:

1 Present age
2 Age of onset of symptoms
3 Duration of relapses, i.e. stays in hospital
4 Duration of latest stay in hospital
5 Type and number of treatments during this stay, including present supportive therapy
6 Diagnosis and prognosis
7 Type of work suggested
8 Any suicidal tendencies

The procedure is said to have worked well. It was instituted because previously two people in the works had menaced their fellow workmen with a sledge hammer and a carving knife respectively, and the company felt that it was only fair to the employees as a community that they should know of any paranoid, murderous, or suicidal tendencies which could be easily concealed in a ten-minute employment interview. (The company must have been unlucky: the statistical rarity of such episodes is discussed in Chapter 6.)

But the majority of those who mention the subject report unsatisfactory experience on the subject of co-operation. The following extracts from respondents' correspondence cover two main areas: first, distrust of the occupational health doctors' role, and consequent unwillingness to divulge information; second, ignorance of, and lack of interest in work rehabilitation and ex-patient employability. On the first subject, one doctor wrote: 'Fantasies about medical staff being agents of the employer, and being less than ethical in their behaviour towards patients, are a significant impediment to helping the patient.' Another:

'I find that there is a reluctance on the part of both patient and doctor to divulge information about the patient's condition and treatment to the medical officer in industry. It seems that the latter's function is widely misunderstood by his colleagues in hospital or in general practice. I have never had a spontaneous approach made to me by any person concerning the return to work and likely work situation of any ex-psychiatric patient.'

Other comments were:

'Family practitioners cover up true diagnoses by writing "hypertension", "nervous debility" etc. on sick note.'
'Extremely difficult to obtain any information about the patient from the consultant psychiatrist, unlike other consultants.'
'Co-operation from hospital consultants given rather grudgingly suggests that the welfare of the patient can often best be served by frankness.'
'We seldom receive adequate or indeed any reports from outside.'

On the second subject, work and employability:

'Consultant psychiatrists and their departments and ancillaries are seldom of any help to me in making a decision about a man's employability.'
'There is still a tendency for departments to ignore the importance of the rehabilitation of an ex-patient in a suitable work situation.'

Such comments point to a quite profound malaise in relations between three groups of medical colleagues, to an absence of confidence more generally associated with a lay-medical relationship. They seem to point also the very real dilemma of confidentiality so frequently encountered in these studies, of which a further example is provided by medical certificates. The Welfare Officer in Case Study Firm B complained that medical certificates never seemed to be received from the neighbourhood psychiatric hospital as they were from the neighbourhood general hospital, no doubt because it was thought improper to divulge a patient's whereabouts to his employer. If the firm thus kept in ignorance were to take the employee's name off the books, they could not in fairness be blamed for it, was the welfare officer's reaction. It looks as if there is scope for a mutually agreed code of procedure to be hammered out between these two branches of the medical profession.

We are now in a position to consider what the comments from these quite numerous employers add up to. As they stand, the extraordinarily varied comments of B employers are perhaps too fragmentary and reflect experience which is too disparate even for meaningful summary. Some things stand out such as the delight of the satisfied employer at seeing ex-patients 'blossom into real people again'. The domestic staff who shopped for the old ladies had evidently settled into an unpressured environment. But the roadsweepers and hospital domestic staff of a few years ago could no longer count on a successful resettlement milieu where one used to be, according to this evidence. And the poor attendance, the difficulties of the first few days, the sheer failure to turn up, are prominent disadvantages to Sample B employers.

For the C sample, it is possible to identify the prevailing ethos among the big organizations with their big medical departments: 'don't take on mentally ill people in the first place if you can help it, but once they belong to the company, treat them with consideration as you would treat an employee who has broken down physically, especially if he has many years' service'. If an employer does not wish to employ once mentally ill people, then the use of a screening questionnaire can ensure that he does not. Job applicants are commonly required to fill in a form asking whether they have ever suffered any mental or nervous trouble, and while an affirmative answer will prejudice the offer of a job, an untruthful negative one will render them liable to dismissal for lying. This was the situation resulting in Mr O'Brien's unsuccessful appeal against his dismissal by the Prudential Assurance Company. Mr O'Brien, competent and successful at his job, had not disclosed his history when asked, and the Prudential's policy not to employ people who had suffered mental illness was, as the law stands, quite legal. There is no doubt in our own minds that many large organizations, including many in Sample C, do their utmost to ensure that no ex-patient is offered any type of employment. The trend of current legislation moreover reinforces the rationality of such an attitude, as our own experience endeavouring to recruit employers for the experimental Southampton Enclave Scheme made clear. The more expensive to the employer become pension, national insurance and redundancy obligations, the more restrictive the legal sanctions involved in employee dismissal, the less sensible is it voluntarily to risk involvement in such situations. Our enclave employers were quite interested in the deficiency payments which were part of the enclave deal, but very much more interested in the fact thay they would not be considered to be the legal employers of an enclave worker.

But once in, the situation of the ex-patient worker in these large organizations was so often quite different, greatly improved. Time and again, the differences between the figures in our I and II schedules (distinguishing old from new employees) exemplified the extent to which allowances are made for long-service workers, both as regards performance and time-keeping. In our D study foremen and supervisors were revealed as possessing often extensive awareness of the nature of ex-patients' difficulties – for instance, one company, anxious to keep on a skilled craftsman who could not bear to be watched while he worked, had the bright idea of building a screen all round him. The medical departments as might be expected were shown as the main centres of support, proffering marriage guidance and advice on family upbringing, health, and diet; and work-oriented themes ranging from career counselling to a change in working hours. Often it was a question of just listening. Systematic follow-up sessions of workers returning after sickness or injury were the speciality of, among others, the Group Medical Officer in our Case Study C. For a workforce of 7,000 he allocated his priorities in such a way as to devote time to, on average, two sessions a week of therapeutic follow-up. A doctor in a large retailing company had become particularly adroit at enlisting the co-operation of departmental managers in keeping their employees out of hospital and at work, involving them in a joint endeavour which she took trouble to explain. In fact managements and medical departments could go to extreme lengths keeping jobs open, overlooking irregularities, and bending the rules.

# 10

## Summary and discussion

Since our research programme was launched in 1970 the entire economy of the industrialized west has suffered misfortunes which have operated unfavourably for disadvantaged workers of all kinds. Overfull employment has succumbed to massive unemployment. Trade unions even talk of sharing out the precious activity. By contrast, evidence, including our own, shows that work has come to be regarded by some as an optional alternative to benefit, sometimes financially unfavourable. From the angle of our concern in this book, perhaps the most significant change is the payment in the United Kingdom of a range of subsidies to perfectly fit and healthy workers, thus driving a coach and horses through early arguments deployed against the principle of subsidising the disadvantaged, though practical difficulties of implementation remain (Department of Employment 1973a: 26–7). Whatever view is taken of all this, whatever degree of intervention in the labour market is accepted, knowledge of the capabilities and weaknesses of different categories of disadvantaged workers is needed if steps are to be taken to assist them more effectively, with or without subsidy. In the case of the mentally ill, this has hitherto been lacking except in fragmentary or anecdotal form, or as derived from studies conducted in laboratory conditions. Our purpose has been to make a start on remedying the deficiency though we are aware that a very great deal remains to be done.

Before attempting to assess the policy implications of our findings it is as well to be reminded what these are.

The starting point in Chapter 1 is that work has been shown to be of clinical benefit to the ex-psychiatric patient when regarded as an aid to rehabilitation. But it can also be something very much more, namely evidence of wellness: achievement of the fully paid-up citizen role.

Approximately how many ex-patients enjoy this status or are actively seeking it is a piece of quantification which we endeavour to supply in Chapter 2.

A review of the principal services concerned with work for the psychiatrically disabled is the topic of Chapter 3. The state services, introduced before the term 'psychiatric disability' was even thought of, have not caught up with the situation resulting from the 1959 Mental Health Act and the chemical discoveries of the same decade. As the years go by, and hospital populations age, they probably never will. But there are signs in the Manpower Services Commission of a determined onslaught on rehabilitation matters following the brilliant consultative documents, while the reforms in the DRO service, and for all one knows, impetus deriving from the personal concern of ministers, may be having their effect.

The voluntary and local authority effort considered in Chapter 3 is openly selective, since we preferred to discuss the principles underlying the success of acknowledged leaders in the field rather than attempt a comprehensive glossary.

The heyday of the industrial therapy units and the ITOs was the late 1950s and the 1960s, when hospitals were discharging their long-stay schizophrenics. Dr Early's first stroke of genius was to jump into the vacuum left by the state services and to provide the length of training needed by these patients. Others followed his lead: scores as regards industrial therapy units funded (as to overheads) by the state; a handful only as regards Industrial Therapy Organizations for which charitable support had to be raised. At the time of writing, the Bristol ITO marks time, its stream of patients reduced to a trickle. Whether this is attributable solely to the stagnant economy, or whether external patients (i.e. referred from sources other than Glenside Hospital) are being referred before their condition is stabilized is a major question to which the answer is not yet clear. Dr Early's second stroke of genius was to create sheltered industrial groups (or enclaves) in the mental illness field; experiment is still required to get the mix in such projects right in present conditions.

A probation officer's experience of the needs of deteriorated and vagrant ex-patients encountered in prison, reception centre, or on the London streets, led Mr Michael Sorensen to formulate the Peter Bedford philosophy. Significantly, he places work first and all other needs, including housing, after. However the contract cleaning available, while unsentimentally organized by a highly qualified professional, allows for variations according to the health and strength of the worker. Where ITOs offered the voluntary organizations' break-through in the 1960s, the Peter Bedford concept could be the pioneering break-through of the 1970s; at least for the deteriorated patient who slipped through the net when the great discharge operation was under way.

The main concern of this book however is with the ex-patient functioning at the opposite end of the rehabilitation spectrum and now holding down an open job. It seemed to us that employment implies two parties, employer and employed, and that hitherto the former have been neglected. Their attitudes are in the first place of paramount importance and they are also able to provide information on ex-patients on a scale, and of a technical definition, not available in employee-based studies however formally perfect. Despite the methodological difficulties indicated in Chapter 4, a series of studies were undertaken with the indispensable active co-operation of employers themselves.

Chapter 4 lies in the professional researcher's province, and indicates the nature of the samples and data which we have been able to obtain. It is worth noting that before the questionnaire survey of 1973 was embarked upon, it was recognised by DHSS, by our Consultative and Advisory Committee and by ourselves, that to obtain a random, representative, national sample would be an impossibility. It was none the less felt that the co-operation of the Society of Occupational Medicine offered the promise of a widely enough based sample for valuable information to be obtained. The unavoidable biases in all our samples are openly discussed.

The bulk of the data describing the actual work currently being performed by members of our open employment samples is assembled in Chapter 5. Analysis by occupation shows the largest category to be that of semi-skilled manual non-machine work. This is larger even than the unskilled category. Clerical grades are also quite numerous. These too are the grades to which employers recruit, when they do recruit, which is extremely seldom. Managerial, professional, supervisory, and technical personnel with a psychiatric history are practically never engaged. An incidental but important finding relates to the C I sample of established employees, and confirms that these normally return to their old jobs after a psychiatric episode.

The data are also considered in relation to other ideas about ex-patients' work. A third of the psychotics in Sample D operate machines: so do many Remploy workers, registered disabled though they be. But overall, machine operation is confined to a minority. Slowness, long identified as a handicap, is confirmed in our studies to be so. The surprising antithesis of manual versus non-manual work was also investigated. While clerical jobs offer work away from the pressure of the production process, small groups in small offices would appear to introduce pressure of a different kind, namely too close social interaction, necessitating above average sickness absence.

Viewing work in terms of role and task offered useful insights into the idea of the overall worker role to which many ex-patients experience difficulty in adapting. However the value of regarding specific jobs in these terms appeared to us less certain. An important finding resulted from investigating the method of introduction, and source of referral of 145 new employees to open employment. Ex-patients referred direct from hospital lasted a shorter time in employment than ex-patients referred or introduced from any other source: friend, advertisement, DRO, employment exchange, or other job. Even a spell of unemployment seemed to offer better preparation. The conclusion was inescapable that the transition from the patient to the worker role, for those straight out of hospital, had been too fast.

This remains one of our most clear-cut results. Consideration of aspects of the social and physical environment of Sample D produced no significant correlations, though the numbers involved were small. Noise and windowless working conditions could not be related statistically to the onset of relapses nor to excessive sickness absence. Strict disciplinary codes were in force where many ex-patients were working without difficulty. Psychotics as well as those diagnosed as depressed or neurotic were to be found in jobs involving face to face contact with the public; 'success' does not according to our evidence appear to be related to these factors.

Nor could success, as measured by our indicators in 1974, be correlated with the operation of trial periods for new employees, nor with consultation with trade unions (quite the reverse!), nor with the practice of reminding ex-patients to take the drugs they had been prescribed. These commonsense measures were applauded by doctor correspondents, but statistical evidence of their effect was lacking. As to the value of professional support, this too, observed in individual instances and thought to be a factor of importance, could not be substantiated statistically.

On the subject of working hours, the variation of which offers the medical officer a useful tool, a clear indication emerged. Overtime was almost universally worked by ex-patients when required, whereas a significant number of them were excused from shift work altogether: evidently shift work presents a trying life-style for the psychologically frail.

Chapter 6 deals with the commonest behavioural deviations observed amongst a minority of ex-patients at work, and considers the incidence and analysis of complaints about slow work, excessive sickness absence, or disagreeable, dangerous, or odd behaviour. Employers' reactions are exemplified in a table showing the association of the three behaviour complaints with continued employment, and show that the rare occurrences of dangerous behaviour are never tolerated; that disagreeable behaviour is barely tolerated; but that oddity of behaviour does not on the figures constitute a significant bar to continued employment.

The excessive sickness absence mentioned by employers as a source of difficulty was exhaustively investigated in our final D study: the findings reported in Chapter 7 confirmed and defined the considerable extent of this problem. A further comparative study however, conducted in a single large manufacturing company, showed that the total sickness absence rate of an ex-psychiatric patient group was little worse than that of a chronic physically disabled group of coronary patients.

Relapses, the cause of another reported difficulty were examined in Chapter 8 from several different angles. They provided data on the phenomenon of downward socio-economic drift and showed that in regard to employed people this is a slow process, for by far the great majority of our sample members returned to their own job after a relapse. Our data included the recording of events at home and at work which could be regarded as potential triggers of such episodes, and yielded interesting profiles comparing the characteristics of ex-patients who suffered relapse with those who did not. On the practical level methods of dealing with relapses were illustrated and discussed.

Finally in Chapter 9, abandoning analytical method, we reported the views of employers who have had experience of employing people with a psychiatric history.

We now discuss the implications of these findings for everybody concerned with them: employers, employees, and the various arms of government.

The key area is that of finding work at all.

The Employment Protection Act is designed to safeguard the position of existing workers, but our research shows that for people with a psychiatric history this is not the main problem, which is to get work in the first place; and this, paradoxically the Act will hinder since, understandably, it will increase employers' reluctance to take a chance.

Once an ex-patient is in work, he is apt to be treated with the same concern with which a physically disabled employee is treated, particularly if he is a long service employee (Meacher (ed.) 1978). The exceptions to this, exemplified in the O'Brien case, are discussed later. Yet despite protestations to the contrary in replies to our questionnaires and elsewhere (e.g. *Personnel Management* January 1979), the majority of employers still try their best to avoid engaging ex-patients, according to our evidence. The tiny recruitment figures in the open employment sample C II point straight to this conclusion. So does the calculation relating to the D sample, about whom it was found that only 16 per cent were known to be ex-patients at the time they were engaged. So do the reported comments in Chapter 9, evidence from John Martin's 'offenders as employees', and from the pressure group MIND, the National Association for Mental Health: indeed so does the evidence of everyday observation.

In our view, and that of certain senior medical officers who have given thought to the matter, blanket exclusions of all ex-patients are wrong and deny to significant numbers of people who are well-recovered and causing no trouble to anyone, the opportunity to earn their living and even maintain their psychological balance. An employment policy intended to embody social justice would ensure that no applicant is turned down on medical grounds unless these make him a source of danger to himself or others. Accordingly, it would safeguard the need to screen for specific occupations of which airline pilot or bus driver are easily appreciated examples. But jobs like this constitute a minority; for the majority of vacancies, in respect of applicants who are not severely ill our view is that employers should chance their arm.

Chance is the word. The element of chance cannot in the present state of knowledge be eliminated, and will persist until the art of assessing employability in ex-patients has improved beyond the promising small-number studies conducted by Bennett, Fraser Watts, and Griffiths. Because of the element of chance, it is hard to see how anti-discrimination legislation on the lines of race and sex legislation, one of the proposals put forward by MIND to the Department of Employment, would help. A person's sex and race is (usually) apparent; not so an ex-patient's employability.

It is important to emphasize, however, the nature of the chance the employer is taking and the analyses presented in the foregoing chapters help to clarify this. An employer risks engaging a potentially poor time-keeper, with, possibly, certain awkward traits, rather than a dangerous maniac as portrayed for dramatic effect on stage or screen. Only 10 per cent of our B and C subjects were complained about for dangerous behaviour, whereas attendance records and spasms of awkward behaviour presented difficulty. By the same token, however, it must surely be the duty of those concerned with placing ex-patients to minimize the risk they are asking employers to accept, and not to submit manifestly unsuitable applicants. Quite a proportion of compassionate

B sample employers had had enough, and were unwilling to chance their arm again.

If an employer has accepted the risk of hiring an ex-patient, he is in our view entitled to expect certain things in return. After the onset of illness, or relapse, in one of his own established employees, with whose welfare our data show him to be much concerned, this employee is almost invariably taken back into his old job provided he can do it, and this, we know also (Shea 1977) is the best thing that can happen to him. But in these circumstances we believe the employer is entitled to expect that the employee will not be sent back to work unrecovered. The data in our D study give cause for concern on this ground. The one factor invariably correlated with onset of illness or relapse in the D subjects is 'Time since last discharge,' indicating that employees most recently out of hospital are those most likely to relapse. The employer, one would think, is also entitled to a much fuller measure of co-operation from National Health Service personnel in hospitals and general practice than he sometimes receives. Such collaboration would include providing information about potential employees, punctiliousness in the matter of sick notes, and co-operation in the event of an emergency involving an employee's immediate removal from the workplace.

If a company has adopted a policy of screening for psychiatric disorder and an employee's psychiatric history, not disclosed at interview, is subsequently discovered, what then? We discussed this with several occupational health doctors in large, reputable organizations before the O'Brien case was heard of. We were assured that in these circumstances no employee would be dismissed though he might be found a different job. In our own research we personally encountered no examples similar to the action of the Prudential Assurance Company in dismissing Mr O'Brien for not disclosing his history, nor that of the Civil Service Commission, a year earlier, in prohibiting the establishment of Mr Michael Lawson (*The Times* April 4 1976). From the literature it is however clear that comparable action is common among employers in the United States. Robert V. Heckel and his co-authors report:

'Once a person has been hospitalised many businesses and industries will hire him under no circumstances. Even when the diagnostic label is indicative of a less severe illness, the fact of hospitalisation causes many insuring agencies to refuse coverage for these individuals . . . some individuals reported that though they concealed their history from their employer, they were fired when it was later disclosed they had been in a mental hospital. Firings occurred even when performance had been highly satisfactory.' (Heckel *et al.* 1973)

This passage may well contain the clue. The common denominator in all three situations is the attitude of the insuring agencies. In the O'Brien case it is the insurance aspect of the Prudential Assurance Company's Pension Fund. In the Lawson case it is the insurance aspect of civil service establishment. In the United States the insurance aspect will also include private cover against workmen's compensation liability, which in the United Kingdom has now been transferred to national insurance (except for action for negligence at common law), as well as whatever pension and sick pay insurances may be present. It is therefore appropriate to ask on what basis insurance companies refuse cover. Are their decisions made on the basis of scientific and actuarial evidence?

## More severely disabled ex-patients: sheltered industrial groups

Though the wholly recovered and the mildly disabled will form the majority of once-hospitalized employees, there will be a group of more severely disabled people to whom the above discussion will not apply. It is likely that members of this group will have been diagnosed as schizophrenic and the evidence assembled from the Industrial Therapy Organization movement, from the government ERCs, and from our own experimental project under the auspices of the Manpower Services Commission, go to show that in their case the rehabilitation process is often a very protracted one. It can be so protracted that the ex-patient may be well enough to work in open industry before he can stand solely on his own two feet. In such cases the device of the sheltered industrial group (or enclave), as pioneered by Dr Early and already mentioned, seems to meet the needs of employer and employee alike; and since the employment department has signified its acceptance of the innovation the great need now is for further adoption of this type of sheltered work.

Since the number of workers engaged in sheltered group work has up to now been tiny (under 150 in January 1976), the arrangement is not well known. It is described below in the terms used by the Disablement Resettlement Service in 1977.

## Notes on enclaves (Sheltered Industrial Groups)

(1) The DE [Department of Employment] Consultative Document on Sheltered Employment (para. 4.13) defined an enclave as 'a

group of severely disabled people working under supervision in an ordinary and undifferentiated working environment'. At present most enclaves are engaged in gardening, general labouring, factory work, street cleaning, and laundry work. While it would be encouraging to see an extension of this type of activity, it would be helpful if progress could be made in developing enclaves in the industrial, clerical and commercial fields.

(2) The conditions for approval of enclave schemes are broadly those which apply to sheltered workshops operated by local authorities and voluntary organizations. Workers in industrial and commercial schemes should have a working capacity of at least one third that of an able-bodied worker. (The level in outdoor schemes should for the time being continue to be maintained at 60 per cent.) In principle the concept involves two organizations. One is 'the firm' in which the group work. The firm provides all that is necessary for their work – space, equipment, amenities, work to be performed, etc. The other is the parent organization which employs or is responsible for the disabled people and which arranges for them to work within the firm. The firm pays the parent organization for the value of the disabled people's output: the employing organization pays their wages and other costs associated with employment, and incurs organizational costs. The parent organization has to meet from other sources any difference between its total costs and the payment it receives from the firm.

(3) The enclave employees should be paid wages by the parent organization. They receive the normal pay for sheltered employees related as necessary to trade rates for the particular work, the parent organization being paid by the firm for the work done. Capitation grant is paid at the rate of 75 per cent in the case of local authority schemes, and 90 per cent in voluntary body schemes, of the difference between the wages cost of the employment of the severely disabled people and the payment by the firm for the cost of the work done, plus the additional costs directly attributable to the administration of the scheme. These costs may include the provision of special supervision or medical attention. The grant is subject to the same maximum as other sheltered employment schemes, i.e. £1400 in 1979.

(4) It is an advantage if the enclave can be operated with a sheltered workshop as a base so that people may progress from the workshop to the more open condition of the enclave. However, an enclave may fill a need in an area where there is an insufficient

number of suitable severely disabled people to justify the setting
up of a workshop.

(5) The number of people to be employed in an enclave will depend
on the type of work to be done. While it is believed that six is the
minimum number for an effective working group there could be
instances where a smaller group might operate more efficiently,
especially in the commercial or industrial field.

Points to remark in this document are that the one-time conditions
that these groups should operate from a sheltered workshop and should
consist of six or more workers are no longer demanded. In fact, in our
experimental Southampton project, no suitable approved sheltered
workshop was at our disposal, and workers were deployed in Dr Early's
famous 'groups of one'.

The advantages of these sheltered industrial groups are wide ranging.
The first is cheapness to the exchequer: the comparative costs of
supporting a sheltered worker in a bricks and mortar workshop, and in
an out-working group have been calculated by ITO Bristol over a ten-
year period as shown in *Table 10(1)*.

Table 10(1)   *Deficiency grant cost per place per year (£)*

|  | 1965 | 1966 | 1967 | 1968 | 1969 | 1970 | 1971 | 1972 | 1973 | 1974 |
|---|---|---|---|---|---|---|---|---|---|---|
| sheltered workshop | 220 | 257 | 275 | 265 | 345 | 358 | 566 | 510 | 784 | 822 |
| sheltered group or enclave | 83 | 128 | 159 | 170 | 200 | 155 | 227 | 267 | 234 | 322 |

The second advantage is to the worker who is enabled to work in 'an
ordinary and undifferentiated working environment' with the avowed
aim of eventual restoration to open employment should this prove
possible. Thirdly, employers, required to pay only for the value of work
performed, are not, under the scheme, employers in the legal sense and
are therefore exempted from worry on the score of Employment
Protection legislation. They as well as the employee, can also look for
support and expertise to a psychiatrically trained nurse supervisor,
whose services are chargeable to centrally funded administration. The
essential prerequisite of this, as of all schemes for rehabilitative or
sheltered employment is a proper degree of assessment for employment.

## The place of the occupational health services

The employer's attitude with regard to the engagement of staff is often
guided by his occupational health doctor if he has one. However, the

extent of the occupational health service's involvement is restricted by two factors; the small numbers of doctors, and to a lesser degree, nurses, in post (*Table 10(2)*); and the breadth or narrowness of the occupational health role envisaged. In the matter of numbers, it will be observed how markedly medical and nursing staff cluster in the larger firms, but, in fact, though they are employed in only 8 per cent of the firms surveyed by the EMAS for their study, these firms employ some 66 per cent of the national workforce. From time to time, particularly in submissions to the Dale Committee (1950) and the Robens Committee (1970), the case has been made for more services to cover the smaller factories, perhaps on a group basis. Seven group occupational health services, all sponsored by the Nuffield Foundation, remain in existence (Hill 1972), and the question may be posed whether they can be organized in such a way as to be of assistance to former patients. We were in touch with several of them, and the longest-established, at Slough, provided notably efficient follow-up arrangements to member firms. On the other hand the members of the Employment Medical Advisory Service, deployed following the Robens Report outside the actual work place, constitute a large force of medical manpower apparently not available for therapeutic counselling.

However, to hold an occupational medical post by no means ensures

Table 10(2)  *Provision of types of occupational health service by size of firm*

| number of employees | % of firms | | | | | | |
|---|---|---|---|---|---|---|---|
| | *medical & nursing staff* | *medical staff only* | *nursing staff only* | *doctor on call only* | *other staff only** | *no service†* | *total* |
| 0–10 | 0.8 | 0.4 | 0.4 | 0.4 | 0.0 | 98.0 | 100.0 |
| 11–24 | 1.2 | 0.5 | 0.4 | 3.8 | 0.9 | 93.2 | 100.0 |
| 25–49 | 0.9 | 1.5 | 1.5 | 7.1 | 2.4 | 86.6 | 100.0 |
| 50–99 | 0.9 | 4.1 | 2.2 | 8.4 | 4.4 | 80.0 | 100.0 |
| 100–249 | 5.4 | 9.8 | 4.9 | 11.0 | 2.6 | 66.3 | 100.0 |
| 250–499 | 22.5 | 9.8 | 14.9 | 6.3 | 7.1 | 39.4 | 100.0 |
| 500–999 | 42.9 | 11.1 | 21.0 | 6.3 | 3.2 | 15.5 | 100.0 |
| 1000–2499 | 78.9 | 4.4 | 7.0 | 3.8 | 0.6 | 5.3 | 100.0 |
| 2500–4999 | 80.0 | 2.5 | 7.5 | 2.5 | 010 | 7.5 | 100.0 |
| 5000+ | 76.9 | 3.8 | 7.6 | 7.7 | 0.0 | 4.0 | 100.0 |

\* e.g. first aiders employed as such for at least 10 hours a week.
† other than first aiders employed as such for less than 10 hours a week.

*Source*: Occupational Health Services, Health & Safety Commission HMSO/1977.

an interest in mental health. For our 1974 study a whole series of statistical tables were assembled in the confident expectation that they would confirm the value of the medical profession in supporting ex-patients. In no way could they be made to show this. While some medical departments, as in Case Study B, provide extensive support, other doctors working on a sessional basis or on call are not in a factory long enough. One doctor confided to us that he had no idea who his ex-patients were, and when invited to take part in the D study, sent a memo to his foremen to find out. Probably, in practice, it will be found to be the occupational health nurse, manning a basic first aid or treatment service, who simultaneously and informally provides counselling as well.

This state of affairs is understandable when it is recalled how successive governments have failed to make up their minds about the whole subject of occupational health. Are doctors supposed to confine their activities to the treatment of injuries and the routine (and time-wasting) examination of job applicants, or do they perform the wider functions of environmental surveillance, preventive work, and re-habilitation, monitoring, and counselling, the very stuff of mental health doctoring? The Robens Committee (on Health and Safety at Work 1972) sheered away from these topics (*Hansard* 30 January 1973: col. 567) and 'concentrated its recommendations upon hazards to health arising from the work place and the job rather than upon the general health care of the individual worker'. A member of the Robens Committee, when asked at a conference why the topic of mental illness had been ignored, replied that it was probably because it was too difficult a subject (Lord Avebury. *Hansard* 30 January 1973 col. 502). It will be appreciated that the wider rather than the narrower in-terpretation of an occupational health doctor's proper field of concern commends itself to anyone who has studied the position of the ex-patient in employment.

## Promotion

At times the most vehement upholders of the rights of mentally ill people castigate employers for alleged 'discrimination' in promotion matters.

Since our own data relate to industrial, commercial and defence organizations they do not touch on members of the professions, nor, except anecdotally, on individuals 'higher' up an industrial hierarchy than the respondent doctors themselves. But in the areas we cover, concern for promotion barely figures. This may reflect the tacit acceptance that decision taking and man management, the essence of the managerial role, are contra-indicated for all but the most completely recovered subjects. Purely technical roles are a different matter. To press indiscriminately for more promotion amongst ex-patients does not appear to us, in the light of our evidence, to be a sensible policy. Rather to obtain a basic job and hold on to it over the long term would seem much more practical. Diagnostic differences seem relevant also. The 1974 analysis of relapses reported in Chapter 8 shows that the few ex-patients who travelled 'up' the socio-economic occupational ladder after a hospital admission had suffered depressive and not schizophrenic illness.

## The arms of Government

It remains to consider whether our findings indicate a need for modification of government policy in relation to mental illness and employment.

The Department of Employment – more precisely the Employment Services Division of the Manpower Services Commission – is the department most concerned. At the time of writing, its rehabilitation facilities for the mentally ill are being actively investigated and experiments monitored. There is a feeling that compared with a few years ago, they have a clearer idea of what they are about. Across the corridor, so to speak, sheltered work has been accepted, or revived, as a potential rehabilitation facility, in suitable, not numerous, but important cases. These are notable gains. But pursuit of the fashionable policy of 'integration' gives cause for disquiet. If by integration is meant the integrated entry of physically and mentally disabled to a facility, there is always danger that the mentally ill will sink to the bottom of the pile: Remploy's record shows this. Not only will they sink to the bottom of the pile, they may be excluded altogether, as in the Peterborough Sheltered Industrial Group or in an approved local authority Sheltered Workshop recently visited. Or mentally ill candidates may be restricted in number for understandable and valid reasons which mean, however, that they are in fact being discriminated against, since the facilities are not numerous enough to accommodate them. Ought official policy, then, to contemplate more specialized facilities for mental illness rehabilitation, rather than off-loading to private charity? The toning-up concept of the ERC is simply not appropriate for a once severely mentally ill person: hence the need for the process to be continued in sheltered work. But this is not generally realized. Parity of esteem, which is desirable as between the mentally and physically disabled, need not imply identity of treatment, which is not.

## The need for assessment

In more than one passage we have deplored the absence of any realistic assessment for employability, a gap which must largely account for past unsatisfactory experiences, and present reluctance to employ, amongst employers. Our own most vivid illustration of this gap derives from analysis of our B II sample.

Certain predictions of employability are now being made by Griffiths and Fraser-Watts on the basis of quite small studies, which could with great advantage be replicated. Other than these, assessments have been made on the basis of trial and error in actual employment, open, sheltered, or rehabilitative: practical-minded nurses and psychiatrists have repeatedly told us that this is the only effective, realistic method yet available. Like the rehabilitation process with which it can be combined, it has to be done over a period, taking time and money. A one-off assessment by a panel on the physical model is useless.

The six months' rehabilitation-assessment period (rightly) required by the Sheltered Work Section of the Employment Services Division before it will grant-aid approved sheltered workers in Industrial Therapy Organizations is not at present funded from central sources and constitutes a heavy charge on charitable funds. As the need for this part of the process has become clearer, so, in our view, has the case for its central funding also, if only to level up – on the parity of esteem argument – the artificial restrictions operated in ERCs.

Though employability assessment cannot yet be regarded as anywhere near an exact science, the art is practised much better in some centres than in others (for reasons discussed in Chapter 1). When the horrific figures of the B II placements came to light, the degree of ignorance among hospital psychiatrists concerning their patients' employability was starkly revealed. If rehabilitation were to be accepted by psychiatrists as a speciality, perhaps courses on employability assessment could be put on in such centres as the Maudsley, Bristol, Reading, Malvern, and Croydon, so that existing insights could be more widely disseminated.

Our other suggestion, to combat the ignorance of the existence and purpose of such facilities as there are, and of the organization of industry, for that matter, would be for short-term cross-postings and long-term joint appointments between related disciplines and different hierarchies. Mentally ill people are still for ever falling between two or more stools. If, as seems sensible, psychiatric hospitals and units are to be regarded as part of a total community provision – rather than ghettos beyond the pale – there seems everything to be said for joint appointments of psychiatrists and clinical psychologists between area health authorities and local authorities. The historical apartheid which has cut off occupational health medicine from the National Health Service similarly needs bridging, probably in this case by training cross-postings, for the ignorance and absence of co-operation between these two arms of the medical profession operate with particular detriment, it appears to us, on the mentally ill employee. In a particular, specialized corner, the involvement of the community psychiatric nursing service, or even perhaps, a specialist social worker, in sheltered industrial groups in open industry can provide backing and know-how where it is most needed. The great need, so far as the health and personal social services are concerned with employment matters, is an awareness of what everybody else is doing.

At the end of the day, whatever administrative adjustments may be made, there will remain a basic question which never faced the authors of the Tomlinson report in 1943: whether the United Kingdom, with over a million unemployed for the foreseeable future, wishes the frailer psychological personalities among us to be helped to retain their sanity by work. As the Manpower Services Commission has commented: 'The Commission will face difficult decisions about the relative priority to be given to measures to safeguard employment opportunities for disabled people, as compared with general anti-unemployment measures.' (Developing Employment and Training Service for Disabled People, para. 2.6)

Does the country want people to be disabled *and* unemployed?

# Appendix 1: Contract between Peter Bedford Trust and participants

The Trust is for people who want to help themselves.

The Trust and its trading company John Bellers Ltd, offer various work possibilities including cleaning, decorating, gardening and training in workshops. The work is arranged so that those who have not held a job for many years may make a beginning at supporting themselves.

The Peter Bedford Housing Association provides accommodation for those who have begun to work on a regular basis and no one can be offered a place to live until they have been in work for at least a few weeks.

Having started working with John Bellers Ltd, or in the Trust's workshops people can change jobs and still keep their accommodation providing they keep to the terms of the licence or tenancy.

The following forms the contract between the individual participant and the Trust. It states those matters that the Trust expects the participant to keep to and what the participant can expect in return.


## 1. The Trust

The Trust undertakes to provide work or training, and accommodation for as long as a person needs them and providing that the individual keeps to their part of the contract.

All new participants will be offered a training opportunity by the Trust within its workshops. . . . Should someone have a particular trade or interest they would like to pursue, then the Trust will try to arrange for it.

A person can earn up to the disregarded income and will then be able to move into part or full-time employment that will leave them better off than if they remained on Social Security.

When someone wishes to get a job outside of the Trust or its trading company, then the Trust will offer whatever assistance is necessary. For example, it will provide a reference for people who have been employed and may be able to arrange an introduction to an employer.

The Housing Association provides everyone with a single room plus the use of a lounge, kitchen and bathroom. The accommodation is secure so long as residents keep to the terms of the contract. Each room will be properly equipped with furniture, bedding, cooking utensils etc., and each house will have cleaning materials regularly provided to ensure that it can be properly maintained. The Association will also ensure that every house is kept in a reasonable condition, bearing in mind that some only have a life of a couple of years.

## 2. The participant

The participant comes to the Trust in order that he or she might earn their own living and run their own lives. The starting point is always a work programme and even when on Social Security, a person will be expected to take part in work training where they will be able to earn their maximum disregarded income – usually £4.00. People will only go back on to Social Security when they have a medical certificate or are unavoidably unemployed. There are no fiddles and no free hand-outs.

Everyone must register with a local doctor and keep in contact with a hospital if this is thought necessary. Sometimes the Trust will hold a person's medication and issue it to them on a daily basis. The Trust keeps a brief record of everyone's medical history and other matters that may be important. Should anyone become ill and refuse to accept medical supervision, then they have to leave because the Trust is not able to look after someone who is very ill.

The residents charge must be paid regularly for accommodation provided by the Housing Association and in the case of people working with John Bellers Ltd., this is usually deducted from their wages. If the rent or charge is not paid, a person will be asked to leave.

Everyone in a house must help in keeping it clean and tidy. Each person has to keep his/her own room clean and to help in looking after the common rooms, kitchen, bathroom and hallways. This will be done through a rota which will ensure that everyone will take their turn at the household chores.

Residents will also be expected to help out with other checks that are designed to ensure people's safety. This can involve the daily checking at each house by the residents themselves to see that no one is ill or in need of help.

Should anyone cause a nuisance that is disturbing to their fellow residents and neighbours, then they may be asked to leave. This includes heavy drinking, physical violence, and the neglect of their household duties.

Signed in acceptance of the terms of the contract:

Participant: ————————————————————————

Peter Bedford Trust: ——————————————————————

Date: ——————————————————————————

# Appendix 2: Work report forms

## Morgan Work Report Form

| A | A Applies | Average | B Applies | B |
|---|-----------|---------|-----------|---|
| 1. Never arrives late or leaves early. | | | | Always arrives late and leaves early. |
| 2. Does complicated jobs. | | | | Can only do simple jobs. |
| 3. Grasps instructions quickly. | | | | Cannot grasp instructions. |
| 4. Works very quickly. | | | | Works very slowly. |
| 5. Works continuously. | | | | Works for short periods. |
| 6. Eager to work. | | | | Avoids work. |
| 7. Looks for more work. | | | | Waits to be given work. |
| 8. Excellent standard of work. | | | | Bad standard of work. |
| *9. Uses tools well   * (See below) | | | | Cannot use tools. |
| 10. Skilful with hands. | | | | Clumsy with hands. |

| | | | |
|---|---|---|---|
| 11. Welcomes supervision. | | | Resents supervision. |
| 12. Needs no supervision. | | | Needs constant supervision. |
| 13. Willing to change job. | | | Refuses to change job. |
| 14. Shows initiative. | | | Shows no initiative. |
| 15. Communicates well. | | | Does not communicate. |
| 16. Always finishes his/her work. | | | Leaves his/her work half done. |
| 17. Gets on well with other people. | | | Gets on badly with other people. |

*9. This includes professional, technical and clerical as well as manual tools.

**Work Report Form from Griffiths (1973)**

| A | A applies | Inclined to A | About average | Inclined to B | B applies | B |
|---|---|---|---|---|---|---|
| 1. Does complicated jobs | : | : | : | : | : | Can only do simple jobs |
| 2. Grasps instructions quickly | : | : | : | : | : | Cannot grasp instructions |
| 3. Works very quickly | : | : | : | : | : | Works very slowly |
| 4. Works continuously | : | : | : | : | : | Works for short periods only |
| 5. Eager to work | : | : | : | : | : | Avoids work |
| 6. Welcomes supervision | : | : | : | : | : | Resents supervision |
| 7. Needs no supervision of his/her work | : | : | : | : | : | Needs constant supervision of his/her work |
| 8. Willing to change jobs | : | : | : | : | : | Refuses to change jobs |
| 9. Looks for more work | : | : | : | : | : | Waits to be given work |
| 10. Always uses good judgement | : | : | : | : | : | Never uses good judgement |
| 11. Excellent standard of work | : | : | : | : | : | Bad standard of work |
| 12. Manual dexterity is good | : | : | : | : | : | Clumsy with hands |
| 13. Uses tools/equipment well | : | : | : | : | : | Cannot use tools/equipment |
| 14. Gets on well with other people | : | : | : | : | : | Gets on badly with other people |
| 15. Communicates spontaneously | : | : | : | : | : | Does not communicate |
| 16. A good timekeeper (punctuality in arriving/leaving) | : | : | : | : | : | A bad timekeeper (no punctuality in arriving/leaving) |
| 17. Always finishes his/her work | : | : | : | : | : | Leaves his/her work half done |
| 18. The others took to him/her quickly | : | : | : | : | : | Doesn't fit in easily |
| 19. Takes a prominent part in things | : | : | : | : | : | Hangs back and lets others take the lead |
| 20. Has a sensible attitude to authority | : | : | : | : | : | Is a bit of a troublemaker |

| | | | | | |
|---|---|---|---|---|---|
| 21. | Were I an employer, I would be very willing to take him/her on | : | : | : | : | Were I an employer, I would prefer not to employ him/her |
| 22. | Is markedly over-confident ('average' means realistic) | : | : | : | : | Is markedly under-confident |
| 23. | Accepts criticism and correction of work readily | : | : | : | : | Cannot accept criticims or correction of work |
| 24. | Accepts responsibilities very readily | : | : | : | : | Cannot really accept any responsibilities |
| 25. | Shows a great deal of initiative (proceeds without instructions, makes own decisions, etc.) | : | : | : | : | Shows no initiative at all (has to be told what to do, given instructions, etc.) |

**Relevant sections of work report form used in current study**

---

4. WHAT WAS THE STANDARD OF HIS WORK?
   Very well turned out                                    1
   Above normal standard                                   2
   Reached an acceptable standard                          3
   Rather sub-standard                                     4
   Of very poor quality                                    5

5. DID THE QUALITY OF HIS WORK VARY
   FROM DAY TO DAY MORE THAN WOULD
   NORMALLY BE EXPECTED
   Yes                                                     1
   No                                                      2

6. WHAT WAS HIS SPEED OF WORK?
   A very quick worker                                     1
   Maintained a normal industrial speed/Produced work
      on time                                              2
   Reached an acceptable tempo                             3
   Slow moving/Sometimes behind with work                 4
   Speed was well below industrial requirements/Always
      behind with work                                     5

7. HOW DID HE COPE WITH INSTRUCTIONS?
   Very quick on the uptake                                1
   Usually grasped a point quickly                         2
   Followed ordinary instructions                          3
   Sometimes failed to grasp a point                       4
   Had to be given simple instructions                     5

8. COMPARED TO OTHERS DOING SIMILAR
   WORK, HOW MUCH SUPERVISION DID HE
   REQUIRE?
   Required much less supervision than others              1
   Required slightly less supervision than others          2
   Required the same supervision as others                 3
   Required slightly more supervision than others          4
   Required much more supervision than others              5
   Not applicable                                          6

10. WHAT WAS HIS INFLUENCE IN THE WORK
    OF OTHERS?
    Showed initiative in assisting others                  1
    Helped others effectively                              2
    Ignored others most of the time                        3
    Sometimes a nuisance to others                         4
    A constant source of disruption                        5
    Worked alone                                           6

11. HOW DID HE RELATE TO OTHERS
    SOCIALLY?
    Painfully self-conscious                          1
    Sometimes self-conscious                          2
    Confident                                         3
    Over confident                                    4
    Bold and insensitive to social feelings           5

12. HOW DID OTHERS RELATE TO HIM?
    Well liked by others                              1
    Liked by others                                   2
    Accepted by others                                3
    Tolerated by others                               4
    Tended to be avoided by others                    5

13. HOW DID HE ACCEPT AUTHORITY?
    Tended to resent authority                        1
    Reserved towards authority                        2
    Reasonable attitude to authority                  3
    Tended to be submissive to authority              4
    Accepted all authority without question           5

14. HOW DID HE CONTROL HIS EMOTIONS?
    Calm, well balanced and emotionally stable        1
    Not easily put out                                2
    Usually well balanced                             3
    Sometimes moody or irritable                      4
    Often very depressed, aggressive or excited       5

# References

Avebury, Lord (1973) *Hansard*. House of Lords. 30 January 1973: col. 502

Benjamin, B. and Haycocks, M. W. (1971) *The Analysis of Mortality and Other Actuarial Statistics*. Cambridge University Press.

Bennett, D. H. (1975) Techniques of Industrial Therapy Ergotherapy and Recreative Methods. In, *Psychiatrie der Gegenwart*. Berlin: Heidelberg Springer-Verlag.

Blauner, H. (1960) *Work Satisfaction and Industrial Trends in Modern Society*. In, W. Galenson and S. M. Lipset (eds) *Labour and Trade Unions*. New York: Wiley.

Bransby, E. R. (1973) Mental Illness and the Psychiatric Services. *Social Trends* **4**: 51–60.

Brown, G. W. and Birley, J. L. T. (1968) Crises and Life Changes and the Onset or Relapse of Acute Schizophrenia: clinical aspects. *British Journal of Psychiatry* **116**: 327–33.

Brown, G. W. and Birley, J. L. T. (1970) Crises and Life Changes Preceding the Onset or Relapse of Acute Schizophrenia: clinical aspects. *British Journal of Psychiatry* **116**: 327–33.

Brown, G. W., Birley, J. L. T. and Wing, J. K. (1972) Influence of Family Life on the Course of Schizophrenic Disorders – a replication. *British Journal of Psychiatry* **121**: 241–58.

Brown, G. W., Carstairs, G. M. and Topping, Gillian (1958) Post-hospital Adjustment of Chronic Mental Patients. *Lancet* 27 September: 685–9.

Brown, G. W., Monck, E. M., Carstairs, G. M. and Wing, J. K. (1962) Influence of Family Life on the Course of Schizophrenic Illness. *British Journal of Preventive and Social Medicine* **16**: 55–68.

Campling, Jo (1976) Getting Back to Work. *New Society* 1 April.

Cheadle, A. J., Cushing, D., Drew, C. D. A. and Morgan, R. (1967) The Measurement of the Work Performance of Psychiatric Patients. *British Journal of Psychiatry* **113**: 501, 841–6.

Clarke, R. D. (1978) Mortality of Impaired Lives 1964–73. *Journal of the Institute of Actuaries* **104**: 1–16.

Cohen (1955) Adjustment of Chronic Mental Patients. *Lancet* ii 684–9.

Department of Employment (1972) *Rehabilitation*. Report of a sub-committee of the Standing Medical Advisory Committee (The Tunbridge Committee). London: HMSO.

—— (1972a) *Resettlement Policy and Services for Disabled People*. A discussion paper. London: HMSO.

—— (1973) *The Quota Scheme for Disabled People*. A consultative document. London: HMSO.

—— (1973a) *Sheltered Employment for Disabled People*. A consultative document. London: HMSO.

—— (1974) *Industrial Rehabilitation for Disabled People*. A discussion paper. London: HMSO.

*Department of Employment Gazette (1972)* Employees in Great Britain mid-1971: an analysis by age, sex, region and industry. June: 535–40.

Department of Health and Social Security (1973) *Mental Health In-patient Enquiry 1971*. DHSS Statistical and Research Report Series No. 6. London: HMSO.

Dubin, R. (1956) Industrial Workers' Worlds: a study of the central life interest of industrial workers. *Social Problems* **3**: 131–42.

Dunham, H. W. (1964) Social Class and Schizophrenia. *American Journal of Orthopsychiatry* **34** (4): 634–42.

Epsom Industrial Therapy Organization *Annual Reports* 1966–75.

Goddard, E. (1976) Report on Sample. In *Social Survey Report 1072: Job Centres*. London: HMSO.

Goldberg, E. M. and Morrison, S. L. (1963) Schizophrenia and Social Class. *British Journal of Psychiatry* **109**: 785–802.

Goldthorpe, J., Lockwood, D., Bechhofer, F. and Platt, J. (1968) *The Affluent Worker*. Cambridge: Cambridge University Press.

Gowrie, Earl of (1973) *Hansard*. House of Lords. 30 January: col. 567.

Griffiths, R. D. P. (1973) A Standardized Assessment of the Work Behaviour of Psychiatric Patients. *British Journal of Psychiatry* **123**: 403–8.

Grimes, J. A. (1978) The Probability of Admission to a Mental Illness Hospital or Unit in In-patient Statistics. From *Mental Health Enquiry for England 1975*. DHSS Statistical and Research Report Series No. 20. London: HMSO.

Heckel, Robert V. and Perry, C. (1973) *The Discharged Mental Patient*.

University of South Carolina Press.

Hill, R. N. (1972) With One Eye on the Accounts: group occupational health services today. *Journal of the Society of Occupational Medicine* **22**: 24–29.

Jahoda, M., Lazarfeld, P. F. and Zeisel, M. (1972) *Marienthal: The Sociography of an Unemployed Community*. London: Tavistock Publications.

Manpower Services Commission (1977) *Developing Employment and Training Services for Disabled People*. An MSC Programme. London: ESA Marketing Services Branch.

Martin, J. and Morgan, M. (1975) *Prolonged Sickness and the Return to Work*. London: HMSO.

Martin, J. P. (1962) *Offenders as Employees*. London: Macmillan.

Mattingly, S. (1978) Disabled Persons Register. *Health Trends* **10**: 19–20.

Meacher, M. (ed.) (1978) *New Methods of Mental Health Care*. Oxford: Pergamon Press.

Miles, A. (1971) Long-stay Schizophrenic Patients in Hospital Workshops: a comparative study of an industrial unit and an occupational therapy department. *British Journal of Psychiatry* **119**: 611.

—— (1972) The Development of Interpersonal Relationships Among Long-stay Patients in Two Hospital Workshops. *British Journal of Medical Psychology* **45**: 105–14.

Ministry of Labour (1943) *Report of the Interdepartmental Committee on the Rehabilitation and Resettlement of Disabled Persons*. (The Tomlinson Committee.) Cmd 6415. London: HMSO.

—— (1956) *Report of the Committee of Inquiry on the Rehabilitation Training and Resettlement of Disabled Persons*. (The Piercy Committee.) Cmd 9883. London: HMSO.

Murphy, J. F. D. (1975) Some Psychological Considerations in Industrial Rehabilitation. *EMAS Third National Conference 1975*.

Olshansky, S. and Unterberger, H. (1963) The Meaning of Work and its Implications for the Ex-mental Hospital Patient. *Mental Hygiene* **45**: 139–49.

Olshansky, S., Grob, S. and Ekdahl, M. (1960) Survey of Employment Experiences of Patients Discharged from Three State Mental Hospitals during period 1951–53. *Mental Hygiene* **44**: 510–21.

Olshansky, S., Grob, S. and Malamud, I. T. (1958) Employers' Attitudes and Practices in the Hiring of Ex-mental Patients. *Mental Hygiene* **42**: 391–401.

Pocock, S. J. (1973) Relationships between Sickness Absence and Length of Service. *British Journal of Industrial Medicine* **30**: 64–70.

Price, W. (1978) Mental Illness: a case for company concern. *Personnel Management* **10** (**12**): 39–42.

Psychiatric Rehabilitation Association (1968) *The Mental Health of East London*. London: PRA.

Remploy (1970) Analysis of Terminations. *Annual Reports (unpublished)*.

Rorsman, B. (1974) Mortality among psychiatric patients. *Acta Psychiatrica Scandinavica* **50**: 354–75.

Shea, M. (1977) Sheltered Employment for Disabled People. Unpublished interim report.

Simmons, O. G. (1965) *Work and Mental Illness: Eight Case Studies*. New York: John Wiley.

Sims, A. and Prior, P. (1978) The Pattern of Mortality in Severe Neuroses. *British Journal of Psychiatry* **133**: 299–305.

Sorensen, M. (1968) Notes for the Bedford Institute Association. September.

Southampton Enclave Team (1978) Fourth Report to Manpower Services Commission (unpublished).

Srole, L., Langer, T. S., Michael, S. T., Opler, M. K. and Rennie, T. A. (1962) *Mental Health in the Metropolis: The Midtown Manhattan Study*, Vol. 1. New York: McGraw-Hill.

Taylor, P. J., *et al.* (1970) A Combined Survey of Chronic Disability in Industrial Employees. *Journal of the Society of Occupational Medicine* **20**: 98–102.

Taylor, P. J. (1974) Sickness Absence: facts and misconceptions. *Journal of the Royal College of Physicians* **8**: 315–33.

Topliss, E. (1975) *Provision for the Disabled*. London: Robertson.

Vaughn, C. E. and Leff, J. P. (1976) The Influence of Family and Social Factors on the Course of Psychiatric Illness: a comparison of schizophrenic and depressed neurotic patients. *British Journal of Psychiatry* **129**: 125–37.

Wadsworth, W. V., Scott, R. F. and Wells, B. W. P. (1961) Employability of Long-stay Schizophrenic Patients. *Lancet* **ii**: 593.

Wansbrough, S. N. (1969) *Contract and Pay Questions*. London: King Edward's Hospital Fund.

—— (1971) *Schemes in Open Industry for the Resettlement of Ex-psychiatric Patients*. Unpublished interim report to DHSS.

—— (1973) From Psychiatric Ward to Shop Floor. *New Society* 19 April.

—— (1974) The Employment of Ex-psychiatric Hospital In-patients: a content analysis of open-ended comment received in recent correspondence with Members of the Society of Occupational

Medicine. *Journal of the Society of Occupational Medicine* **24**: 130–3.

—— (1975) Up the Enclaves. *New Society* 27 February.

Wansbrough, S. N. and Cooper, P. J. (1977) Psychiatric Diagnosis in Relation to Some Aspects of Employment. *Journal of the Society of Occupational Medicine* **27**: 50–57.

—— (1978) The Effect of Psychiatric Hospital Admission on Persons in Employment in England and Wales. *Social Psychiatry* **13**: 219–29.

Wansbrough, S. N. and Miles, A. (1968) *Industrial Therapy in Psychiatric Hospitals.* London: King Edward's Hospital Fund.

Watson, E. E. (1967) Industrial Casework. *Transactions of the Society of Occupational Medicine* **17**: 109–13.

Weinberg, S. and Kirson, E. (1968) *The Sociology of Mental Disorders.* London: Staples Press.

Whitehead, F. E. (1971) Trends in Certified Sickness Absence, in *Social Trends* 2. London: HMSO.

Willcox, B. R. C., Gillen, R. and Hare, E. H. (1965) Do Psychiatric Out-Patients take their Drugs? *British Medical Journal* **2**: 790–92.

Wing, J. K. (1977) The Management of Schizophrenia in the Community. Lecture to the American College of Psychiatrists, Atlanta, Georgia.

Wing, J. K. and Brown, G. W. (1970) *Institutionalism and Schizophrenia: A comparative study of three mental hospitals 1960–68.* Cambridge: Cambridge University Press.

Wing, J. K. and Hailey, A. M. (1972) (eds) *Evaluating a Community Psychiatric Service: the Camberwell Register 1964–71.* London: Oxford University Press.

Wing, J. K., Bennett, D. H. and Denham, J. (1964) *Industrial Rehabilitation of Long-stay Schizophrenic Patients.* Medical Research Council Memo No. 42. London: HMSO.

Wooton, B. (1959) *Social Pathology and the Concept of Mental Health.* London: Allen & Unwin.

Wright, B. (1975) *Executive Ease and Disease.* London: Pan Books.

# Name index

# Subject index

For Product Safety Concerns and Information please contact our EU
representative GPSR@taylorandfrancis.com Taylor & Francis Verlag GmbH,
Kaufingerstraße 24, 80331 München, Germany

Printed and bound by CPI Group (UK) Ltd, Croydon, CR0 4YY
08/05/2025
01864439-0003